Institutional Change, Discretion, and the
Making of Modern Congress

Institutional Change, Discretion, and the Making of Modern Congress

An Economic Interpretation

Glenn R. Parker

Ann Arbor
THE UNIVERSITY OF MICHIGAN PRESS

Published in the United States of America by
The University of Michigan Press
Manufactured in the United States of America

1995   1994   1993   1992   4   3   2   1

Library of Congress Cataloging-in-Publication Data

Parker, Glenn R., 1946–
    Institutional change, discretion, and the making of modern
Congress: an economic interpretation / Glenn R. Parker.
        p.   cm.
    Includes bibliographical references and index.
    ISBN 0-472-10329-6
    1. United States. Congress. House.   2. Legislators—United
States.   3. Legislative bodies—Economic aspects.   I. Title.
JK1331.P37   1992
328.73′072—dc20   92-5631
                                                                CIP

To those who have traveled on a sea of thought alone

Acknowledgments

I would like to acknowledge the following scholars who offered encouragement and helpful suggestions during the course of this research: Suzanne Parker, William Bianco, Tom Dye, Richard Fenno, Jr., Morris Fiorina, James Gwartney, Leroy Rieselbach, Kenneth Shepsle, and Gordon Tullock. I want to thank Florida State University for awarding me a sabbatical to undertake training in public choice and Robert Tollison and James Buchanan for making my stay at the Center for Study of Public Choice (George Mason University) a valuable learning experience. I also want to express my appreciation for the time and attention devoted to this project on the part of my research assistant, Jill Kosiewski, and my secretary, Harriet Crawford. Special thanks are owed to my graduate and undergraduate students, whose healthy skepticism about the application of economics to legislative behavior spurred me to write this book. Like most authors, I am deeply indebted to the reviewers of this manuscript, Scott Ainsworth and Barry Weingast, for providing so many thoughtful suggestions and giving the book such a careful reading. I am equally indebted to Colin Day, Director of the University of Michigan Press, for his helpful advice and assistance in preparing this book for publication.

Contents

Introduction

One of the most fascinating features of the Congress of the United States is how it has changed during the past two centuries from a part-time legislature to a coequal, if not at times dominant, partner in government some two hundred years later. And the changes are indeed dramatic: party voting has declined, electoral safety has increased, the perquisites of office have grown, legislative committees have been permanently altered, congressional careers have lengthened, legislative power has been progressively decentralized, and controls on the ethics of members are more exacting than ever before. Despite the rather profound nature of many of these changes, little attention has been given to explaining how and why Congress has evolved in the manner that it has. Two major exceptions to this generalization are the theories proposed by Lawrence Dodd and Nelson Polsby.

Explaining the Evolution of Congress

Dodd (1985) suggests that legislators are driven by a desire for individual power to decentralize institutional influence within Congress; then, as power dispersal weakens institutional power, thereby devaluing individual influence, attempts are made to recentralize power in order to augment the eminence of Congress. This cycle operates in the following fashion:

> At the outset, when politicians in a quest for national power first enter Congress, they decentralize power and create committee government. Decentralization is followed by severe problems of congressional decision making, presidential assumption of legislative prerogatives, and an eventual presidential assault on Congress itself. Congress reacts by reforming its internal structure . . . eventually, however, problems of internal congressional leadership and coordination will become so severe that Congress will be forced to take centralizing reforms. . . . As the immediate threat to congressional prerogatives recedes, members of Congress . . . become preoccupied with their immediate careers and press once again for greater power dispersal. (Dodd 1985, 500)

An alternative explanation is proposed by Polsby, who suggests that Congress (the House of Representatives, to be precise) has become *institutionalized* over time. An institutionalized legislature exhibits the following characteristics:

> 1) it is relatively well-bounded, that is to say, differentiated from its environment. Its members are easily identifiable, it is relatively difficult to become a member, and its leaders are recruited principally from within the organization. 2) The organization is relatively complex, that is, its functions are internally separated on some regular and explicit basis, its parts are not wholly interchangeable, and for at least some important purposes, its parts are interdependent. There is a division of labor in which roles are specified, and there are widely shared expectations about the performance of roles. There are regularized patterns of recruitment to roles, and of movement from role to role. 3) Finally, the organization tends to use universalistic rather than particularistic criteria, and automatic rather than discretionary methods for conducting its internal business. Precedents and rules are followed; merit systems replace favoritism and nepotism; and impersonal codes supplant personal preferences as prescriptions for behavior. (Polsby 1985, 82)

These two theories have become accustomed ways for interpreting how and why Congress has changed in certain directions rather than others. This book offers another perspective on the question of the evolution of Congress— an economic interpretation. This perspective relies upon concepts and theories in microeconomics for insights about the evolution of Congress, concepts and theories which have been ignored in past treatments of congressional change.[1]

My model incorporates propositions and concepts related to principal-agent theory; when applied to the study of Congress, legislators are viewed as agents of constituents and parties (or party leaders speaking on behalf of the party). The underlying question in principal-agent relationships is how to ensure that agents act in the best interests of their principals rather than in their own self-interest or, from the perspective of this study, the degree to which legislators follow the dictates of constituents and parties. In short, who do members of Congress represent? I contend that legislators are relatively free to ignore the wishes of constituents and party leaders because of the existence of barriers to entry (into Congress) and the costs of policing the behavior of legislators. In fact, members of Congress behave as if they were trying to maximize their own discretion. This premise accounts for many of the

---

1. For a good, brief discussion of many of the economic concepts used in this analysis, see Caves 1977, Maurice 1986, or Moe 1984, especially 750–58.

changes over time in the major forces shaping the modern Congress, as well as the behavior of today's legislators.

The premise that members of Congress seek to expand their discretion does more than explain the evolution of Congress as a political institution; it also provides additional insights into the motivations of legislators. In this regard, the study joins the works of David Mayhew (1974a), Morris Fiorina (1977), and Richard Fenno, Jr. (1973), in identifying factors that motivate legislative behavior. Mayhew's contribution to this literature is not only his recognition of the importance of reelection to members of Congress, since this premise occupied the place of a truism for years before the publication of *Congress: The Electoral Connection;* rather, Mayhew's astute observation about how this motivation has shaped the organization of Congress, affected the formation of public policies, and molded the internal and external behavior of members served as a catalyst for the development of rational choice models of legislative behavior.

Fiorina's *Congress: Keystone of the Washington Establishment* provided a critical impetus to the further development of rational choice explanations of congressional behavior; he introduces a theory that ties the reelection of legislators to a rational web of relationships among bureaucratic agencies, interest groups, and legislative committees—the so-called cozy triangle phenomenon (Parker 1989, 199–215). According to Fiorina, members of Congress trade support for agency budgets (and the expansion and protection of these budgets) for programs and bureaucratic fix-it services beneficial to constituents. This mutually beneficial relationship leads to increases in the federal budget and the number of electorally safe members of Congress.

One of the major criticisms leveled against these two seminal works is that they exaggerate the centrality of reelection to the actions of legislators. This argument is supported by Fenno's classic study, *Congressmen in Committees.* In this work, Fenno claims that members of Congress are motivated by three factors: getting reelected, formulating "good" public policy, and gaining legislative power and influence. Fenno then demonstrates that these three concerns motivate legislators to formulate rules (strategic premises) for committee decision making that further these goals.

Institutional Change, Discretion, and the Making of Modern Congress: An Economic Interpretation combines some of the most notable features of these works. The simplicity of the assumption of discretion-maximizing politicians parallels the parsimony associated with the reelection assumption. Moreover, the organization of Congress, the behavior of legislators, and the nature of public policy can be linked to a discretion-maximizing, as well as a reelection-motivated, legislature. Finally, discretion-motivated legislators are driven by a broader panoply of goals, not merely reelection; hence, this assumption captures the multidimensional goals that find expression in legislative behavior. The theory also takes on a challenge that is not addressed by these three seminal works—namely, explaining the evolution of Congress as a political institution.

Assumptions and Models of Congress

Despite the enormous amount of research conducted on Congress, most scholars, political analysts, and journalists would agree that it remains difficult to understand the forces that drive the institution and the behavior of its members. This is not the fault of legislative scholars since considerable effort has been expended in studying *all* facets of congressional behavior. As a direct result, we have accumulated a large inventory of facts about Congress and the legislative process. (See, for example, Parker 1989; Loewenberg, Patterson, and Jewell 1985.) What seem to be lacking in this ever-expanding literature are parsimonious ways to understand what motivates members of Congress.

The public choice literature offers an unusually attractive model that combines simplicity with predictive power, along with a healthy measure of skepticism about politicians. In most treatments of legislative behavior incumbent legislators are assumed to be motivated by reelection. That is, they seek to maximize reelection, or their margins of victory. This model has generated a variety of predictions and considerable research.[2] My analysis offers an alternative to the reelection motive—namely, that members of Congress act as if they were trying to maximize their own discretion.[3] This assumption maintains all of the virtues of the reelection premise and explains elements of congressional behavior and the evolution of Congress that remain unexplained by the reelection motive (e.g., altruism and the advancement of nonparticularized causes and legislation).

It might be suggested that the assumption of discretion-maximization produces hypotheses so similar to those derived from the assumption of a reelection-motivated legislature that it is impossible to distinguish between them. Clearly, some behavior on the part of discretion-maximizers could masquerade as reelection-motivated behavior. For instance, the efforts of legislators to create barriers to entry may reflect an interest in reelection or a desire to create a reservoir of electoral support sufficient to sustain discretion-

---

2. The volume of research that uses the reelection assumption is too lengthy to mention even in part. Some of the most widely cited are Downs 1957; Mayhew 1974a; Fiorina 1977; Arnold 1979; Ferejohn 1974; Stigler 1971; Weingast 1979; Weingast, Shepsle, and Johansen 1981; Peltzman 1985; Weingast and Marshal 1988; Niskanan 1971; and Shepsle 1978.

3. For a provocative analysis of bureaucratic behavior using the maximization of bureaucratic discretion as a major assumption, see Niskanan 1971.

ary actions in Washington. There are, however, instances where the hypotheses derived from these two assumptions predict widely divergent behavior. For example, interest groups confronting a discretion-maximizing legislature "pay" incumbents for the favors they have provided in the past, while in a reelection-motivated legislature those "contributions" are designed to promote reelection. That is, whether groups pass money to legislators to help in their reelection campaigns or as remuneration for past service helps to distinguish hypotheses derived from the reelection assumption from those based upon discretion-maximization.[4] Similarly, the reelection assumption might account for congressional careerism in terms of the growth of electoral safety, while the assumption of discretion-maximization would imply that the growth in the opportunities for individual legislators to exercise discretion underlies the lengthening of congressional terms of service. Legislators motivated by reelection vote to further group or constituents' interests; those motivated by discretion give greater expression to their own personal predilections. Other distinctions could be identified, but I feel that these examples are sufficient to demonstrate that the motivational impetus of reelection and discretion can yield contrasting predictions.

The reelection motive might be preferred to discretion-maximization because it sounds like the type of assumption that mirrors the democratic values in society. Reelection, after all, is the linkage that keeps politicians in line: those who don't serve their constituents well have short legislative careers. Moreover, the desire for reelection should make politicians unusually sensitive to the wishes and opinions of voters.

Models based on the reelection assumption have produced conclusions, however, that almost make a mockery of the operation of representative government, at least in terms of how our textbooks often characterize the process. The costs of information, for instance, restrict voters' knowledge of the candidates and their stands (rational ignorance), thereby reducing constituents' control over their representative, and weakening a major condition for representative government.

Propositions drawn from principal-agent theory also give us cause to worry about the extent to which legislators ignore the best interests of their constituents in order to benefit themselves. Members of Congress can be viewed as agents of constituents who act as principals in the same way managers of firms relate to stockholders. The difficulty in monitoring the behavior of agents defines an important issue in public choice, microeconomics, and studies of legislative representation: how can the principal maintain control over an agent? The inability of constituents (principals) to

---

4. There is empirical evidence that groups contribute to congressional incumbents in exchange for political favors, not to influence election outcomes (Welch 1980).

monitor the behavior of their legislators (agents) limits their control over them.

One conclusion reached by assuming rational behavior on the part of reelection-motivated political parties is that the behavior of these parties intentionally confuses voters by increasing the difficulty of voting on the basis of issue positions—a basic consideration in (rational) voters' calculations of their own utility (Downs 1957). That is, the rational behavior of a reelection-oriented political party (i.e., a party that seeks to maximize votes or chances for reelection) leads to irrational behavior on the part of voters:

> competition forces both parties to be much less than perfectly clear about what they stand for. Naturally, this makes it more difficult for each citizen to vote rationally; he has a hard time finding out what his ballot supports when cast for either party. As a result, voters are encouraged to make decisions on some basis other than the issues, i.e., on the personalities of candidates, traditional family voting patterns, loyalty to past party heroes, etc. But only the parties' decisions on issues are relevant to voters' utility incomes from government, so making decisions on any other basis is irrational. (Downs 1957, 136)

The reelection assumption has also given new meaning to the *organization* of Congress: it is designed to promote the reelection of its members (Mayhew 1974a; Weingast, Shepsle, and Johansen 1981; Weingast 1979). "If a group of planners sat down and tried to design a pair of American national assemblies with the goal of serving members' electoral needs year in and year out, they would be hard pressed to improve on what exists" (Mayhew 1974a, 81–82). Congressional committees, staff, Capitol Hill offices, and the congressional parties themselves are arguably structured to promote electioneering.

The promotion of particularized legislation is another conclusion reached by scholars assuming a reelection-motivated legislature. Mayhew sees particularized benefits as sharing two properties: each benefit is given to a specific person, group, or constituency with a single member of Congress as the recognized provider, and each benefit is distributed in an ad hoc fashion with the incumbent playing a role in the allocation (1974a, 54). The emphasis on particularism results in the strong tendency for legislators to wrap policies in packages that are salable as particularized benefits. In short, not only do members of Congress aggressively seek out opportunities to supply particularistic benefits to their constituents but they tend to frame laws to give a particularistic cast to matters that do not obviously require it:

> Thus in time of recession congressmen reach for "accelerated public works" bills listing projects in the various districts; presidents prefer

more general fiscal effects. In the education field a congressional favorite
is the "impacted areas" program with its ostentatious grants to targeted
school districts; again presidents prefer ventures of more diffuse impact.
(Mayhew 1974a, 128)

The reelection motivation has also led scholars to conclude that members
of Congress pay unusual attention to the opinions and demands of organized
groups (Stigler 1971; Downs 1957). Anthony Downs, for example, contends
that governments construct policies "often aimed more at the good of a few
voters than at the good of all, or even a majority" (1957, 93). The government
listens to organized groups in society because of the intensity with which they
press their claims, and because the party in power needs the resources supplied by these groups to convince voters to return it to power at the next
election (see, for instance, Stigler 1971). To acquire the money and resources
for reelection, the government sells favors to those who need government
action and are willing to pay for it.

A reelection-minded legislature develops a hearty appetite for one of
Congress's least-attractive preoccupations: the penchant for pork-barreling.
Most scholars analyzing Congress from the reelection perspective link reelection to the supply of district benefits at the expense of the federal budget. As
Barry Weingast and his colleagues note, "legislators are reelection oriented
and . . . their prospects are positively associated with the next benefits they
deliver to their constituents" (Weingast, Shepsle, and Johansen 1981, 652).
Because of the specificity of the project and the diffuseness of the costs
(shared by all taxpayers, even those not receiving the direct benefit), legislators have incentives to allocate funds for inefficient projects—pork-barreling.

William Niskanan (1971) makes a similar argument. Niskanan contends
that legislators gravitate to those committees that provide the greatest benefits
to their constituents. The result is that those legislators whose constituents
have the greatest demand for the services and programs supplied by a committee dominate committee decisions. By allocating large shares of the federal
budget to projects favored by committee members and allotting a less bounti-
ful share of the budget for non–committee members less in need of such
projects, the committee is able to pass a large number of inefficient projects.[5]
Constituents benefit even though they have to pay the costs of these projects
because their share of the cost will be less than the actual cost of the project,
which is shared by all taxpayers. This produces net benefits for constituents—
an important component in reelection victories.

Finally, the reelection motive provides a rationale for the growth of
government. Fiorina (1977) argues that the reelection motive has given legislators incentives to expand the federal bureaucracy. The expansion of govern-

---

5. For an effective critique of Niskanan's model, see Miller and Moe 1983.

ment means the expansion of federal programs; hence, more benefits can be delivered to constituents and credit taken (or claimed) for the provision. There is another way in which the expansion of government is linked to the reelection motivation: legislators gain electoral support because the greater the scope of government activity, the greater the demand for legislators' services, and the more voters will appreciate those services. Therefore, legislators have strong incentives to expand the bureaucracy since it puts more voters in need of legislators' "unsticking services."

The process, according to Fiorina, works something like this. Members of Congress earn electoral support by establishing various federal programs. The legislation for these programs is drafted in very general terms so that some agency of government must translate this vague mandate (i.e., the intent of Congress) into functioning programs; as a consequence, numerous rules and regulations are promulgated that produce errors of commission and omission. Angered constituents bring the matter to the attention of their legislators, who are sympathetic and successfully intervene on behalf of constituents. This system produces an ever-expanding bureaucracy and an electorally safe membership:

> The bureaucracy serves as a convenient lightning rod for public frustration and a convenient whipping boy for congressmen. But so long as the bureaucracy accommodates congressmen, the latter will oblige with ever larger budgets and grants of authority. Congress does not react to big government—it creates it. All of Washington prospers. More and more bureaucrats promulgate more and more regulations and dispense more and more money. Fewer and fewer congressmen suffer electoral defeat. Elements of the electorate benefit from government programs, and all of the electorate is eligible for ombudsman services. (Fiorina 1977, 49)

It should be clear that the democratic-inspired assumption of reelection-motivated politicians has resulted in a variety of provocative characterizations of Congress; such caricatures stir the ire of many who study the institution. Simply put, the reelection motive has produced unflattering characterizations of Congress and the behavior of its members, what Charles O. Jones refers to as "slam-dunk" explanations of congressional behavior!

Few would deny that the reelection motive has produced some rather unsavory characterizations of Congress and its members: Congress is populated by individuals interested only in getting reelected, not serving the public interest. Moreover, Congress listens most intently to those who provide electoral resources, usually economic interests; not surprisingly, economic, rather than social, interests are normally cultivated by an electorally motivated legislature. Inefficiency means little to reelection-minded legislators when deciding public policy; raids on the federal budget are a congressional pastime.

True or not, and most empirical studies have tended to support these propositions, such conclusions emphasize the most negative aspects of congressional behavior. Are there no virtues to the performance of Congress and its members? Perhaps a different assumption, such as discretion-maximization, would lead legislative scholars to probe features of Congress that would yield more positive, or more balanced, conclusions about the institution.

The assumption of discretion-maximization may incur resentment and opposition because it seems too cynical, à la Chicago Political Economy, with its emphasis on wealth transfers (Tollison 1989), or perhaps seems too undemocratic. Assumptions should not be viewed as biasing predictions toward certain conclusions; if they do so, it is only because assumptions raise certain questions that lead scholars to look in some places rather than others for answers to these questions. Assumptions are only tools of inquiry, serving as analytic devices to generate hypotheses in the study of some phenomena; their value depends upon the uses to which they are put. Granted, some assumptions are more congruent with basic societal norms or democratic principles, but it is impossible to determine a priori whether or not an assumption will yield democratically pleasing conclusions. (Can any assumption yield conclusions more cynical than those associated with reelection?) In any event, the assumption of discretion-maximization yields testable hypotheses and its utility depends upon how well it illuminates the political process.

The assumption that legislators act as if they were trying to maximize their own discretion is not intended to foster a skeptical view of what motivates legislators; rather, this assumption, in addition to yielding empirically valid descriptions and explanations of congressional behavior, unearths conclusions about Congress that place the institution in a far more favorable light. Moreover, the favorable aspects of Congress's operations, such as altruistic voting (voting in the public interest rather than in the parochial interests of one's constituents), are just the types of activities that are left unexplained by the reelection motive but can, nonetheless, be explained by the assumption of discretion-maximization. Thus, the discretion-maximization assumption is a powerful tool for understanding Congress, explaining some behavior that the reelection motive fails to predict, and generating hypotheses that are less cynical than the conclusions reached by the reelection assumption *but equally valid*. The discretion-maximization assumption is not expected to replace the use of the reelection assumption, but only to serve as a plausible alternative. In sum, this analysis is guided by the assumption that legislators seek to maximize their own discretion. Like most assumptions, this one is not subjected to empirical verification, although evidence of legislators being motivated by power, ideology, and altruism can be found throughout the literature on Congress. The underlying research question is, if members of Congress are intent upon expanding their own discretion, how would they behave?

Principals, Agents, and Team Production in Legislatures

This study explores an important economic relationship with direct application to politics: the principal-agent relationship.[6] An agency relationship is a contractual agreement under which one individual (or more)—the principal—engages another individual—the agent—to perform some service on the principal's behalf. This, of course, involves delegating decision-making authority to the agent. If both parties to this relationship are utility-maximizers, there is good reason to believe that the agent will not always act in the best interests of the principal. The principal can limit divergence from his or her interests by establishing incentives for the agent to conform to the principal's preferences and by incurring monitoring costs designed to limit the aberrant activities of the agent.[7] This problem—inducing an agent to behave as if he or she were maximizing the principal's welfare—is quite general, existing in all organizations and in all cooperative efforts, from universities to labor unions.

Voters, constituents, groups, and party leaders are the ultimate principals in the legislative process, and members of Congress are their agents. A major problem inherent in, and disruptive of, the principal-agent relationship is the exercise of discretion: discretion occurs when agents pursue their own interests while ignoring the preferences of their principals. A natural remedy for this problem is to invest resources into monitoring the agent's actions, especially since issues such as moral hazard create a divergence between the principal's interest and the agent's actions.[8] It is costly, however, for princi-

---

6. For an interesting analysis of the application of principal-agent theory to the study of congressional-bureaucratic behavior, see Weingast 1984.

7. The essence of the principal's problem is to design an incentive structure so that the agent—with his or her own interests at heart—is induced to pursue the principal's best interests. Since information about the agent's actions is likely to be both imperfect and skewed in favor of the agent, the design of an efficient incentive structure must include monitoring systems as well as mechanisms for inducing the agent to reveal his or her privately held information.

8. Moral hazards arise from "an asymmetry of information among individuals that results because individual actions cannot be observed" (Holmstrom 1979, 74). The term *moral hazard* is usually used to describe conditions arising in risk-sharing situations where the private actions of the insured affect the outcomes; normally moral hazards are discussed in analyses of insurance against uncertain events (Arrow 1970; Spence and Zeckhauser 1971; Kihlstrom and Pauly 1971). My use of the term in the discussion of Congress is inspired by Weingast and Marshall's description of a form of moral hazard arising in the exchange of IOU's:

the first legislator may claim that he can no longer support the bill and so attempt to renege. Since the state of the world is observed only by one legislator, it is difficult for the second

pals to monitor the actions of their agents since the full observation of actions is either impossible or prohibitively costly:

> Political institutions, and legislatures in particular, are likely to possess many of the attributes that make the policing of policymakers by their constituents imperfect. These attributes include attenuated constituent ownership shares; the absence of easily enforceable contracts between constituent-principals and their legislator-agents; likely impediments to competition; and free-rider incentives afflicting potential monitoring by constituents. These attributes do not imply that policymakers are not monitored and policed. Rather, policing and monitoring need only be costly to lead us to expect that constituents do not select the corner solution of perfect control over their agents. (Kalt and Zupan 1990, 107–8)

This reduces the incentives for rational legislators to follow district (constituents') or party interests.

It should be clear that the maximization of discretion is a means to various ends. In this sense, discretion-maximization functions like profit-maximization: it serves a number of ends and is a prerequisite for achieving most of them. Legislator discretion finds expression in many different ways. For instance, voting in the public's interest rather than the interest of the district and ideological legislative behavior are clear expressions of individual preferences (Kalt and Zupan 1984, 1990; Kau and Rubin 1979). It might be suggested that discretion needs to be defined with greater precision so that empirical testing and inquiry can proceed more easily. Such a demand is not within the scope of this inquiry, nor am I certain that high levels of precision can be obtained. My objection to attempting such closure is unrelated, however, to the feasibility of defining discretion more precisely. I believe that the utility of discretion to legislators rests on just this breadth: discretion provides many types of benefits that legislators value; hence, the fact that such a term encompasses many types of activities, from rent extractions to altruistic voting, makes discretion all the more valuable to legislators and explains the widespread demand to acquire it.

In addition, there is no reason to believe that the vagueness surrounding the meaning of discretion is an obstacle to inquiry. In fact, just the opposite conclusion might be reached: the demand for exactness of meaning can have a pernicious effect on inquiry, fostering the premature closure of ideas. "Tolerance of ambiguity," Abraham Kaplan writes, "is as important for creativity in science as it is anywhere else" (1964, 71). Moreover, to say that the term discretion is too vague is not to diagnose a weakness but, at most, only to

---

legislator to verify the first's claims about whether he should be required to hold up his end of the bargain. (1988, 140)

report a symptom since all theoretical terms are vague to some degree. Again, such vagueness is not an impediment to inquiry:

> The vagueness of our terms does not consist in the fact that we are continually confronted with the problem of "where to draw the line," but in the fact that we cannot solve this problem beforehand and once and for all. The point is that lines are drawn and not given; that they are drawn always for a purpose, with reference to which the problem is solved in each particular case; that our purpose is never perfectly served by any decision; and above all, that no decision can anticipate the needs of all future purposes. Every term directs a beam of light onto the screen of experience, but whatever it is we wish to illuminate, something else must be left in shadow. (Kaplan 1964, 66)

My arguments should not be construed as encouraging deliberate vagueness in the construction of concepts or theories, or even a modest degree of apathy toward its occurrence. I would only contend that we are fooling ourselves to believe that all can be defined away and that scientific inquiry always benefits from such precision.

The exercise of discretion poses problems for legislative leaders because it is disruptive of team production, such as the production of legislation. Legislatures can be viewed as populated by teams of legislators, or political parties, who organize and compete to produce legislation; here, there are incentives for rational individuals to exert a less-than-expected or normal productive effort—*shirking*. Shirking is one of a class of behaviors that reflects the exercise of discretion. The term *team production* refers to a situation where the combined costs of identifying the marginal productivity of individual team members, and compensating them accordingly, are high. Thus, in the absence of mechanisms for monitoring each individual's behavior, team members cannot be rewarded according to their specific individual impacts on the output (e.g., legislation). In this setting, individual team members have incentives to exploit their discretion to shirk, thereby free riding on the work of others and not being penalized for it:

> Each individual knows that his effort has some impact on the team's reward, but that this reward is split among all members; thus, while he bears the full cost of his effort, he receives only part of what his effort produces. On the other hand, when he shirks by reducing his effort expenditures, the savings in effort accrue only to him, and the resulting losses in team reward are borne largely by others. A fundamental asymmetry therefore characterizes the structure of incentives, and each member will tend to find it in his own best interests to engage in some degree of shirking. (Moe 1984, 750–51)

I normally use the term *shirking* to describe those conditions that encourage legislators to neglect (or renege on) their responsibilities in the production of legislation (e.g., trading work for leisure). Legislator shirking is just one expression of the exercise of discretion; that is, all shirking reflects the exercise of discretion, but the exercise of discretion may occur without legislator shirking.[9]

In conclusion, the value of assuming that legislators seek to maximize discretion is that it leads to the study of congressional behavior from a perspective that would normally escape the notice of most congressional researchers. It leads us to address different questions (e.g., how discretion influences the behavior of party leaders and the formation of public policy), and it provides new answers to old questions (e.g., why congressional careers have lengthened). Finally, the maximization of discretion yields useful insights into the motivations of legislators and the historical evolution of Congress.

Description of Data and Chapters

The data for the empirical part of this study are drawn from public records describing the operations and structure of the House of Representatives between 1881 and 1988. While the starting point for this analysis has no real temporal significance, it does serve several useful purposes. The Forty-seventh Congress (1881–82) is a good starting point for several reasons. First, this Congress allows us to establish electoral and congressional conditions prior to the turn of the twentieth century, when many fundamental changes in the nature of Congress were precipitated (for example, the institutionalization of the seniority system began in the early 1900s). Second, the Forty-seventh Congress differed in size from Congresses that followed;[10] this assures variation in an important variable in economic explanations of legislative behavior (see, for instance, Stigler 1976). Third, this Congress predates the 1896 realignment so that the effects of an important natural barrier to entry can be examined and compared to the efforts of legislators to contrive to raise the barriers to entry even higher. Finally, information about Congresses before 1880 is difficult to obtain through standard library efforts such as interlibrary loan. For these reasons, then, the analysis spans the last century in the House of Representatives (1881–88).

In chapter 1, I lay the basic groundwork for the theory and later empirical

---

9. For instance, a legislator who votes his or her own conscience is exercising discretion, but if that vote is consistent with district opinion, no shirking has actually occurred.

10. The House of Representatives grew from 332 members in the Forty-seventh Congress, to 357 legislators in the Fifty-second Congress, then again grew to 391 representatives in the Fifty-seventh Congress, and to its present size of 435 members since the Sixty-second Congress.

analysis: I describe the evolution of natural and contrived barriers to entry into Congress and how they enabled members to expand their existing levels of discretion. In chapter 2 how discretion-maximizing behavior occurs in legislatures is examined, and the expansion of discretion in the House of Representatives between 1881 and 1988 is analyzed. The role of party leaders in the model is explored in chapter 3; here, I examine the effects of discretion in reducing team spirit and therefore party loyalty and the effect of expansions in discretion on the productivity of Congress.

Economic incentives to congressional service are explored in chapter 4. The focus of this chapter is on the question of why careers in the House have lengthened over time. My theory suggests that the expansion of discretion is an attractive feature of congressional service and an incentive to establish long careers in Congress; I examine this hypothesis along with several other economic propositions that link service in Congress to economic benefits and the capacity to shirk due to the costs of monitoring. Chapter 5 is devoted to a discussion of how discretion-maximization is kept within effective limits and an examination of the relevance of durable rules constraining legislative discretion.

Chapter 6 is a summary of the arguments made and the major components of my theory of discretion-maximization. In this chapter attention is also given to the derivation of some testable hypotheses drawn from the theory and the empirical analysis contained within the study. I conclude with a discussion of how recent changes in Congress during the past decade affect my arguments and how representation occurs in a discretion-maximizing legislature.

Some may feel that I have pushed this idea too far or failed to give adequate attention to other equally tenable hypotheses and theories. I admit to doing so; however, I have not acted out of ignorance but because I believe that all scholars should ride their ideas as hard as they can and leave it to others to hold them back. While there is no reason to believe that my emphasis will preclude the exploration of alternative explanations, there is every reason to suspect that the controversial nature of the premise of discretion-maximization will discourage investigation; hence, my emphasis seems warranted if only to ensure that adequate consideration is given to the argument that legislators, if not all politicians, seek to maximize their own discretion. This is not intended to precipitate an argument over the advantages and disadvantages of discretion-maximization in Congress. I only demonstrate the value of this motivation in explaining legislative behavior and accounting for the evolution of Congress.

CHAPTER 1

Barriers to Entry and the Expansion of Discretion

Economic models are based on the assumption that people are motivated by self-interest. Economic theories of Congress normally add the assumption that legislators seek to maximize their electoral support or likelihood of reelection. This analysis retains the assumption of self-interest but replaces the reelection motive with a different assumption: legislators seek to maximize their own discretion. While the reelection assumption leads us to look for evidence of electioneering in the activities of legislators, the assumption of discretion-maximization leads us to look for evidence that members are intent upon expanding their discretion—giving greater rein to their own preferences and predilections. In the following chapters, I demonstrate the value of viewing legislators as striving to expand their existing levels of discretion and the insights into legislative behavior that result.

The basic premise of this study is that discretion-maximizing legislators create barriers to entry into Congress that yield large vote surpluses; the resulting electoral safety provides legislators with monopoly-like profits that translate into latitude and discretion.[1] So as not to squander these profits, legislators demand and create systems of rules to protect their ability to exercise discretion without the fear of interference on the part of their party leaders. Once established, these rules encourage legislators to invest scarce resources into their work and careers within the legislature. As confidence in the security of, and returns from, these investments rise, members willingly expand their areas of discretion.

Barriers to Entry

Barriers to entry diminish electoral competition by enhancing the advantages of incumbency and deterring quality candidates from challenging incumbents.[2] (For a different but compatible discussion of barriers to entry, see

---

1. There is a nice analogy between the development of vote surpluses, the exercise of discretion, and the personal bank account: vote surpluses are deposits into the incumbent's bank account, and the exercise of discretion represents withdrawals from that account. I am indebted to William Niskanan for suggesting this point.

2. It has become almost a truism that incumbents win frequently and by large margins of victory because they face nominal competition. From the perspective of this study, it is not the

Tullock 1965.) Barriers to entry can arise from legal requirements (e.g., licenses and patents), economies-of-scale that prevent competition from small organizations, and control over an essential resource. Neither legal restrictions nor economies-of-scale appear to create overly restrictive barriers to entry into Congress, but the last condition—control over an essential resource—underlies an important set of barriers to entry: contrived barriers. Contrived barriers result from the actions of legislators that intentionally or unintentionally reduce competition. Entry barriers can also be natural, created as by-products of political and social events over which legislators have remote, if any, control. Two examples clarify the distinction: electoral realignments and the expansion of government subsidies.

The electoral realignments of 1860, 1896, and 1932 had the effect of reducing competition by establishing electorally safe areas (Brady 1988); for example, as a result of the 1896 election, the Northeast was made safe for Republicans and the South for Democrats—conditions that would persist for decades. On the other hand, the enormous increases in office perquisites during the 1960s and 1970s (table 1) were incumbent-created advantages that reduced electoral competition by enabling incumbents to expand the market for their services and reduce the elasticity of demand. It might be argued that realignments reflect the efforts of congressional incumbents to create regional pockets of electoral safety, but this seems unlikely, though some natural barriers to entry may also have artificial qualities. This distinction is designed only to guide the reader through the explication of the theory.

Natural barriers to entry arose to create fertile conditions for exercising discretion in Congress: the 1860, 1896, and 1932 realignments created widespread electoral safety. The profits obtained from increased electoral safety could not be spent with discretion because of the influence of party leaders who set strict constraints on the legislative behavior of their members.[3] Once rules were devised to restrict the intervention of party leaders into the affairs of their members, incumbents began to expand their discretion. For example, the electoral safety created by the 1896 realignment reduced membership turnover in the House of Representatives and led to the adoption of an informal rule designed to enhance the discretion of legislators by reducing the influence of party leaders over the careers of their members: the seniority system (Price 1975; for an alternative explanation for the rise of seniority, see Polsby, Gallaher, and Rundquist 1969). Discretion expanded at a modest rate, at first, reflecting the uncertainty associated with electoral safety and investing

---

present incumbents per se that deter capable competition but the barriers they have erected over time.

3. For a discussion of the dominant role of party leaders in early Congresses, see Cooper and Brady 1981.

TABLE 1. **Increases in House Perquisites, 1945–75**

Specific Allowance	1945–60	1961–75
Clerk hire (number of staff)	5—1945	9—1961
	6—1949	10—1964
	7—1954	11—1966
	8—1955	12—1969
		15—1971
		16—1972
		18—1975
Postage (dollars per session for airmail and special delivery)	90—1945	500—1963
	125—1952	700—1968
	200—1954	910—1971
	300—1957	1,140—1974
Telephone and telegraph (units)	40,000—1959	45,000—1962
		50,000—1963
		70,000—1967
		80,000—1970
		100,000—1973
		125,000—1975
Travel allowance (round trips per session)		2—1963
		4—1965
		12—1967
		18—1973
		26—1975

Source: Data from Committee on House Administration.
Note: These separate allowances were consolidated into the Official Expense Allowance in 1978.

time in legislative careers. As members gained greater confidence in the security of these investments, and greater control over their electoral destinies (aided by government-subsidized advertising), they expanded their areas of discretion.

Just as the effects of earlier barriers were beginning to erode (for example, long-standing areas of electoral safety were becoming more competitive), others arose. Barriers to entry were raised again in the 1960s and 1970s as government subsidies for incumbent advertising increased (see table 1). This enabled members of Congress to increase the size of their markets (voters) and intensify consumer preferences for their services: the advancement and protection of the interests of constituents. Members of Congress accomplished this by differentiating their services to constituents—claiming *personal attention* and producing evidence of just such a personal touch (visits to the district). This made the demand for their service less elastic (i.e., intensified voter preferences), guaranteeing larger and safer reelection victories. Voters' high opinions of their legislators and their low opinions of others serving in Congress is evidence of the success of incumbents in differentiating their products and creating an inelastic demand for their services (Parker and Davidson 1979).

Economists refer to the *elasticity of demand* as indicating the degree of responsiveness of the consumption of a product, or its purchase, to variation in price. More generally, elasticity measures the relative responsiveness of one variable to a change in another. An elastic demand means that buyers (consumers, voters, and constituents) are relatively responsive to changes in price, whereas an inelastic demand occurs when buyers are unresponsive to such changes. The term is used here to describe the extent to which constituents are loyal, or committed, to a particular legislator; where demand for a legislator's services are inelastic, the legislator can depend upon a reliable core of supporters regardless of the degree of shirking and discretion that is uncovered through monitoring. If, in contrast, the demand is elastic, a legislator pays a heavy price in terms of constituents' support when his or her transgressions are unearthed. Where the demand is elastic, the smallest error in judgment or behavior may cost a legislator dearly in the next election. Clearly, legislators benefit when there is an inelastic demand for their services; hence, their activities are directed at reducing the elasticity of demand.

The most important determinant of demand elasticity is the availability of substitutes. Simply put, when good substitutes for a product are available, a price rise simply induces consumers to switch to other products (demand is elastic). For instance, if the price of one brand of toothpaste rises, many customers respond by switching to a different brand. The task facing legislators, therefore, is to convince constituents that there are no good substitutes. They accomplish this task by differentiating their products from potential competitors (challengers). As I noted, showering personal attention on constituents is one way in which members of Congress differentiate their products and thereby promote the perception that there are no good substitutes for their services to constituents. Later in this chapter I describe how such product differentiation occurs. At this point I only want to suggest that members differentiate their products in order to reduce the attractiveness of substitutes (those who might challenge an incumbent's reelection) and thereby create a reliable core of supporters who are not easily enticed away.

The ability to *advance and protect the interests of constituents* places incumbents in a unique position, resulting from their monopoly over bureaucratic fix-it services and the production of legislation (Fiorina 1977). It is the control over these resources that has been exploited by legislators through increased advertising. The growth in incumbent advertising increased the demand for the maintenance of constituency services, regardless of the cost to constituents in terms of potential shirking or the exercise of discretion (i.e., policymaker independence)—by-products of electoral safety and longevity in office. Incumbent advertising, subsidized by government, has raised the barriers to entry even higher, enabling many legislators to increase their electoral safety and therefore their ability to exercise discretion in Washington.

The change in home styles (i.e., the ways in which legislators cultivate their constituents) that started in the mid-1960s reflected a change in product advertising (Parker 1986; Fenno 1978): an emphasis on *personal contact* with "customers" (constituents) subsidized at the government's expense.[4] Such personal contact builds voters' confidence in their legislators and creates a stable following of supporters (Parker and Parker 1989). Fiorina (1977) offers an intriguing alternative hypothesis. According to Fiorina, legislators have altered their style of representation (how legislators behave in, and toward, their districts) to emphasize the delivery of constituency services. In contrast, I contend that the most significant change in style of representation is a change in *product advertising,* not a change in the product per se. Fiorina also sees legislators as shifting emphasis from the more controversial aspects of their job—lawmaking—to nonprogrammatic concerns such as constituency service.[5] In my theory, the relationship is reversed. That is, members of Congress have become more interested in lawmaking, not less. It is, of course, impossible to demonstrate that legislators in the past pursued constituency service with the same fervor as today's legislators, especially given the technological changes that have expanded production possibilities with respect to the delivery of district services, but there is evidence that levels of personal contact—a change in how legislators advertise their services as well as themselves—have increased (Parker 1986). There is also impressionistic evidence that legislators in today's Congress perform the same types of services

---

4. Members of Congress do indeed spend considerable time attending personally to constituent business. John Saloma III estimated that more than one quarter (28 percent) of a representative's average workweek is devoted to constituency affairs and a similar amount of the legislator's staff time is also spent on constituency matters (25 percent) (1969, 184–85). More recent data suggest an even higher percentage of time may be devoted to constituency affairs, since a large proportion of a legislator's time in Washington, as well as in the district or state, is spent on constituency matters. About one-third of the average day of senators is spent in Washington dealing with constituents' mail or talking with constituents or groups (U.S. Congress, Senate 1973, 28), and members of the House devote a similar proportion of time to district affairs while in their Washington offices (U.S. Congress, House 1977b, 18–19). In the district or state, almost all of a legislator's time is taken up with presentations to constituents, and he or she spends considerable time there: representatives spent about one of every three days in their districts, while senators spent one of every four days in their states in 1980 (Parker 1986).

5. In the second edition of his book, Fiorina (1989, 91–93) accounts for the paradoxical growth in lawmaking activity with some of the same cost-shifting mechanisms noted here and elsewhere (Parker 1986). However, why legislators would emphasize the more controversial aspects of the job when their only interest is reelection remains unaddressed.

that legislators in past Congresses offered constituents. That is, the factor that distinguishes the constituency service of today's legislator from those in the past relate more to the level of personal contact than to the type of services provided.

A Historical Perspective on Constituency Service:
A Change in Product Advertising

Putting the issue of volume aside, constituency service has not changed very much in the last two hundred years except for a change in how that service is advertised—increased personal contact between legislators and their constituents. Some of the similarities in constituency service are evident in the circulars that incumbents mailed to their constituents in the late 1700s and early 1800s. Circular letters reported on the proceedings of Congress and national affairs and were periodically sent to constituents by members of Congress, generally those representing southern and western districts. This practice, begun in the First Congress, survives today in the form of slickly produced congressional newsletters and mass mailings. Most members of Congress hoped that these circular letters would be regarded by voters as an acceptable substitute for individual, personal letters; at the same time, they expected that a single copy of a circular letter would be read by more than one constituent. Circular letters provide an indication of what members wanted constituents to know, and what members thought they wanted to know.

It is not surprising that the messages contained in circulars sound similar to those promulgated through today's newsletters. Diana Evans Yiannakis (1982) found that present-day newsletters and press releases tended to emphasize the members' positions on national issues; circular letters also provided information about a legislator's positions on pressing issues. Circulars, like newsletters, were also written to achieve maximum political benefit. Many circulars reminded voters that the incumbent was again a candidate for reelection, and some members even managed to have their letters arrive at politically opportune times. Congressman John Clopton from Virginia, for example, explained his inability to write a longer letter to his wife by noting that "I have been so closely engaged in getting circular letters ready to go by this mail to be in time to arrive at the election for New Kent next Thursday that I have barely time to drop you a few lines" (Cunningham 1978, 429).

Unlike present-day mass mailings, few circulars were directed toward local concerns, but a trend in that direction became evident by the third or fourth decade of the nineteenth century. Letters of members from newer areas, mainly western, indicate members were significantly more concerned with matters relating directly to the local interests of their constituents than those of members from the older, largely southern, states. The available circular letters written by territorial delegates suggest that such persons looked upon themselves largely as lobbyists for their respective territories. The territorial delegate confined his or her activities in Congress mostly to matters concerning territories, particularly his or her own, and reports to constituents tended to be an account of how the legislator had looked out for their interests.

Circulars also conveyed the same type of home messages that members of Congress deliver today. For example, Matthew Lyon's April 1808 circular to his Kentucky constituents called attention to his ability to identify and empathize with constituents in much the same way as Fenno's legislators (1978):

> Whatever advocation I have pursued, I have never ceased to be a farmer, since I have been a man. Very few persons in the district have raised more corn and wheat, and done more labor with their own hands, than I have with mine. No man can better sympathize with, or know the feelings of the laboring man, than myself. Although I do some mercantile business with and for my children, my property is such as is common to the other people of the district. I can have no interest different from yours. (Cunningham 1978, 600)

And like today, early representatives were eager to run errands for constituents. For instance, James Kolbourn of Ohio noted his willingness to help constituents in an 1815 circular: "If any of my constituents have claims upon the government, requiring to be presented at the public offices, they will please to command me, accompanying their accounts, with proper vouchers and instruction, and the best that circumstances will permit, it will be my pleasure to do on their behalf" (Cunningham 1978, 906). Such errands covered a multitude of issues, some of which continue to occupy the attention of members of Congress and their staffs. John Scott's list of accomplishments, addressed to his constituents in the Missouri Territory in the early 1800s, bears more than a faint resemblance to the problems handled by present-day congressional offices:

> There had been committed to my charge during the last two sessions that I have been the delegate, upwards of one thousand individual applications for redress, composed of soldiers' applications for patents, soldiers and militia pay, applications for pensions by disabled soldiers, and the widows' half-pay pensions, claims on government for supplies furnished troops, for property lost and destroyed during the war, claims growing out of Indian depredations, Indian agencies, Indian treaties and supplies furnished at the same, private applications on land subjects, and other claims on the justice or bounty of the government. (Cunningham 1978, 1986)

Representatives in the early Congresses also pursued constituents' complaints with the same dogged persistence exhibited by today's legislators. William Lattimore's 1815 circular to his constituents in the Mississippi Territory is one example of just how tenacious these early legislators could be in handling constituents' requests and complaints:

> Having received, too late in the session for legislative relief, a petition from a number of the inhabitants of Wilkinson County, praying to be secured from a forfeiture of their lands, I laid it before the Commissioner of the General Land Office, with a letter of my own stating the circumstances of the territory, and the unsatisfied claims of the people for military services, and soliciting a suspension of the sales of lands which are or soon may be forfeited; and having been afterwards informed that the subject was still under the consideration of the secretary of the treasury, to whom it had been referred, I called on him, and received a very satisfactory expression of his disposition to grant the indulgence solicited, provided he should find that he could do it on legal grounds. (Cunningham 1978, 936).

Even then, the bureaucracy served as a convenient whipping boy for members of Congress:

> When I am canvassing my district and I come across a man who looks distantly and coldly at me, I go cordially to him and say, "My dear friend, you got my printed letter last session, of course?" "No sir,"replies the man with offended dignity, "I got no such thing." "No!" I cry out in a passion. "No!! Damn that post-office!" (Cunningham 1978, xix)

While it is impossible to know how pervasive these themes and messages were in earlier eras, it is clear that some incumbents did indeed display the same type of behavior that we associate with constituency service today. Members of Congress, past and present, picture themselves as qualified, capable of identifying and empathizing with constituents, and worthy of trust. They seem prepared, if not willing, to explain their positions and votes to constituents; they are vigilant over the interests of their districts and constituents. Despite such similarities, there is one way in which district service in the early years differed from that of today: how it is advertised—the allocation of *personal* time to constituents.

There is no way of directly calculating exactly how much time legislators in the early Congresses spent with their constituents. It seems likely that the time members spent in their districts and states was inversely related to the length of legislative sessions in the early years of the Republic. Members stayed in Washington only as long as they needed to; time not spent in session was normally spent in the district or state (and traveling between the constituency and Washington). "Almost none of the members acquired homes in the capital or established year-round residence there. They merely wintered in Washington, spending more time each year with constituents than with each other" (Young 1966, 89).

Furthermore, Washington was not a very attractive place to spend time because it served as a "magnet for society's idle and society's unwanted: people sick in mind or body, imagining conspiracies against them, imploring help, or bent upon revenge; pleaders for pardons and reprieves; small-time confidence men; needy pamphlet-writers, selling their talents for calumny for the price of a public printing contract; . . . most conspicuously of all it was the indigent who migrated to Washington" (Young 1966, 25). For these reasons, then, the longer the legislative session in early Congresses, the less time spent with constituents. By this measure, past legislators spent considerably more time in their districts and states than present members of the House and Senate.

Since most members now maintain a second home in Washington, time spent in the district or state means even more time spent away from families. Therefore, the close of a legislative session no longer automatically leads legislators to return to their districts or states as in earlier eras. Today's senators and representatives actually spend less time in their districts and states between legislative sessions and Congresses than in the past (Parker 1986).

Prior to the 1960s, high levels of constituency contact were rather unusual and largely structured by a member's position in the seniority hierarchy. Writing in the 1950s, Donald Matthews characterized the personal attention of senators to their constituencies as following a seniority-based political life cycle:

> If the senator survives the first challenge to his position, then he becomes more secure than before. All the advantages he possesses at his first reelection bid are even more compelling now. But with greater seniority and security go additional legislative responsibilities. By the end of his second term, he is, in all likelihood, a senior member of major committees. He is well on the way to becoming an important national figure, increasingly concerned with pressing national and international problems. In the vocabulary of social psychology, his "reference groups" change, he becomes more concerned with Senate, national, and international problems, and devotes less time and attention to the folks back home. The press of legislative duties becomes ever harder to escape. Advancing years make fence-making trips increasingly onerous. (1960, 242)

Since the mid-1960s, however, the amount of time *all* incumbents (House and Senate) spend in their constituencies has increased (Parker 1986). Today's legislators, regardless of seniority, appear to have reversed a trend that has characterized the personal contact of incumbent legislators since the turn of the century: members are spending more, rather than less, time in their districts and states.

Congress supplied some of the incentive for the increased personal contact with constituents by reducing the direct costs associated with constituency attention. Some of this cost reduction was accomplished by increasing the subsidies for various constituency activities and expanding the perquisites available for maintaining contact with constituents. For example, as the subsidies for constituency travel were increased, representatives spent more time in their districts.

Other costs were made more transferable by shifting them to staff: office staffs were enlarged and charged with greater responsibility for constituency service. This enabled members to expand their services to constituents without having to bear the full brunt of the increased contact. Thus, the use of staff for constituency service helped members to shift most of the burden of such activities without reducing the level of service to constituents. No matter how many staff assist them, legislators still claim all the credit for the provision of constituency services, and who can credibly dispute those claims.

Another means of reducing costs was to structure the legislative schedule to allow members to spend time in their districts and states without detracting from the more appealing demands of their Washington activities (e.g., committee work). By structuring the legislative schedule so that members could spend time with constituents without jeopardizing legislative interests, Congress helped to reduce the opportunity costs of such attention. Perhaps the most obvious way in which Congress structured the legislative schedule to reduce these costs is through the proliferation of recess periods. Congress normally conducts no legislative business during recesses; hence, legislators need not worry about forsaking legislative interests or responsibilities while spending time with their constituents. Some recess and holiday periods, such as the one-month recess during August of the first session of every Congress, are even dictated by legislative statute.

The legislative schedule has been modified in other ways to facilitate personal contact with constituents. Congress, especially the House, is infamous for operating on a Tuesday through Thursday schedule of business, which enables members to spend their weekends in their constituencies—a good time for maximizing contact with constituents. Blocks of time have also been set aside in the legislative schedule for constituency visits and travel (i.e., district work periods). Since most business in the Senate is conducted under unanimous consent agreements, scheduling decisions in the Senate are as accommodative to members as are those in the House, which also helps to reduce conflicts between legislative business in Washington and time spent in the senators' states.

Members of Congress played an integral role in promoting the widespread change in constituency contact. They pressured their leaders to make the legislative schedule more amenable to the demands of constituency travel. They established various federal subsidies that reduced the costs associated with increased personal contact, and they consistently supported the expansion of these office perquisites. Even the expansion of the legislative workload and the increase in constituents' demand for services might be construed as occurring at the behest of members of Congress (Johannes 1980).

The cumulative effect of these actions was an interlocking and reinforcing set of incentives that made personal contact more attractive, feasible, and rational. Subsidies for constituency travel, for example, would be useless unless time could be created within the legislative schedule for district visits; congressional recesses and the Tuesday–Thursday legislative schedule provided ample opportunities for exploiting these travel allocations. Increasing constituents' demands makes no sense unless the cost of such expanded service can be easily absorbed; consequently, increases in staff made the expansion of constituency service viable for many legislators. The interlocking of these incentives was achieved as incumbents modified institutional arrangements to facilitate constituency contact.

These institutional incentives were coordinated (interlocked) as a result of the serial and remedial manner in which legislative decisions are made. Charles Lindblom (1965) called attention to the ability of Congress to coordinate disjointed legislative policies by dealing with problems in a serial (sequential) fashion and by rectifying errors of commission and omission that result from the decisions and actions of others. In short, by acting remedially and serially to deal with the adverse consequences of previous decisions (i.e., attending to neglected consequences), policies become coordinated. Thus, as Congress sought to remedy the problems that legislators had in taking advantage of one incentive, it actually created additional incentives that both reinforced and complemented existing ones. For instance, Congress steadily increased the travel allowance so that more of the costs of the travel would be borne by the federal government, but without relaxing the demands of the legislative schedule, members could not easily take advantage of the spiralling subsidy. One way to deal with this problem was to modify the legislative schedule to accommodate the needs of members to spend time in their districts without jeopardizing legislative interests; hence, recess periods were increased and blocks of time within the legislative schedule were established for travel to the district or state. Modifying the legislative schedule remedied some of the problems involved in exploiting the travel allowance while reinforcing the incentives for members to spend time with constituents. As these efforts accumulated, powerful sets of incentives were created.

The effects of cost subsidization and modification of the legislative schedule in promoting attention to constituencies are reflected in the changes in the amount of time that House and Senate incumbents personally spent in their districts and states. I assembled a time series of the monthly travel of House and Senate incumbents compiled from travel vouchers filed with the clerk of the House and the secretary of the Senate between 1958 and 1980; these data were subsequently coded in terms of the mean number of days per month spent in the constituencies. The analysis of these data indicates that increases in the House and Senate travel allowances, and the proliferation of recesses, significantly increased the time legislators spent in their states or districts (Parker 1986).

Incumbent Advertising as a Barrier to Entry

There are two general types of advertising: informative and image advertising. Purely informative advertising generally conveys pertinent price and quality information (e.g., food store ads), while image advertising is designed to make consumers associate the advertised image with the consumption of the product or service. The purpose of informative advertising is to lower the search cost of potential purchasers of the product in the expectation that these people will purchase the advertised product. Image advertising has two related goals. First, such advertising is designed to make consumers think that other products are not good substitutes for the advertised good. Second, image advertising makes the demand for a product less elastic.

It should be obvious that image advertising corresponds quite well to the type of activities that legislators undertake: presenting an image of an individual attentive and responsive to the needs of constituents (Fenno 1978). Indeed, the penchant for legislators to "run against Congress" in their reelection campaigns and during visits to their districts can be viewed as attempts to lead voters to believe that incumbents' replacements will not do as well in looking out for districts' interests as the present officeholders. By attacking others, and calling attention to the "bad guys" in Washington, incumbents elevate themselves and their services in the eyes of constituents. Their services become prized commodities. As a consequence, we tend to see our own legislators as unique— unlike the others, who are viewed as corrupt, lazy, and out for self-gain. This is one way that legislators differentiate their products—themselves—from those supplied by competitors.

In general, there are at least three ways in which personal contact helps legislators to differentiate their products. First, the mere contact enables legislators to claim greater personal attention than their predecessors and all other competitors; there is no better example of personal attention than actually spending time in the district. Second, the contact provides opportunities for legislators to issue quality assurances to their constituents. These quality assurances take the form of the basic home-style messages that legislators shower on their constituents: "I can empathize with your plight; I can identify with your interests; I am qualified to serve" (Fenno 1978).[6] These messages differentiate legislators from other politicians who are normally viewed as far less competent, hardworking, or worthy of trust (Parker and Davidson 1979; Parker 1989b), and the messages help to alleviate constituents' fears of legislator shirking (Parker and Parker 1989). Finally, personal contact enables legislators to distance themselves from their parties and leaders by running against Congress while visiting their constituencies. This helps legislators to escape the blame for institutional and policy failures.

There are a variety of findings that support this conclusion. For one thing, we tend to see our own legislator as better than most others and to evaluate him or her higher than the collective body (Fenno 1975; Parker and Davidson 1979). We also have greater confidence in our own legislator but have little faith in the actions of Congress or its leaders (Lipset and Schneider 1983). And legislators themselves are frequently observed bashing the institution (Fenno 1978). It is not hard to understand why constituents are so reticent about turning incumbents out of office: they fear that the successors will not supply the services that the incumbents could always be counted upon to deliver. In this way, incumbents differentiate their products, reduce the attractiveness of substitutes, and intensify constituents' preferences. In the process of advertising, incumbents stir up business and increase the demand for their services. Higher demand means greater profits for the producer—the legislator—that can be turned into increased discretion.

The ability of incumbents to provide services to constituents acts as a barrier to entry since only incumbents can provide the services and gain recognition for doing so. In fact, constituents are virtually silent about the constituency attention of those who challenge incumbents but quite vocal about the constituency service supplied by incumbents (Parker 1986). This is one characteristic that differentiates between candidates to the advantage of incumbents and because most service receives high marks from constituents, the provision of services improves the standing of members of Congress in their districts. Thus, the monopoly over bureaucratic fix-it services raises a barrier to the entry of new members.

The fact that most of the costs associated with the advertising of these services are subsidized by the government (table 1) raises the barriers to entry

---

6. For a description of the messages that members of Congress deliver personally to constituents, see Fenno 1978.

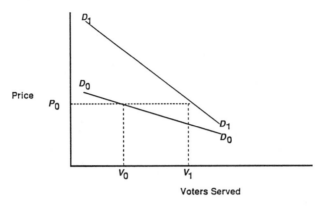

Fig. 1. The effects of advertising on demand for service

even higher by increasing the costs of campaigns for those challenging incumbents. Incumbents can campaign on a daily basis and be paid while campaigning, the legislative schedule is adjusted so that time spent in the district does not detract from legislative interests, and the resources needed for the purpose of advertising are subsidized by the government. Not only have incumbents cornered the market on ombudsmen services for constituents, but the advertising and provision of these services are also subsidized by the government!

Increased advertising enabled members of Congress to increase the demand for their services and reduce the elasticity of that demand. As the market for the legislators' services expanded, monopoly-like profits in terms of increased electoral safety resulted (fig. 1). The decline in elasticity intensified constituents' preferences for incumbents and assured a reliable core of supporters and safe election margins. The gain in electoral safety created margins of political capital that incumbents could spend with discretion.

How increased advertising yields greater profits for members of Congress in terms of increased discretion is depicted in figure 1. The demand curve $D_0 D_0$ represents the demand for an incumbent's services with existing advertising. At the price set by the incumbent, P_0, he or she will serve V_0 voters and gain their votes. The extent to which the gain in votes translates into electoral safety creates monopoly-like profits that the legislator can spend with discretion.

Now increased advertising of the incumbent's services increases demand and shifts it outward to $D_1 D_1$. This shift in demand enables the incumbent to capture V_1 votes (or voters) and increase his or her existing level of electoral safety. Notice also that future price increases (for example, more legislator shirking) will have less of an impact on the demand for the incumbent's services with increased advertising ($D_1 D_1$). This ensures incumbents a de-

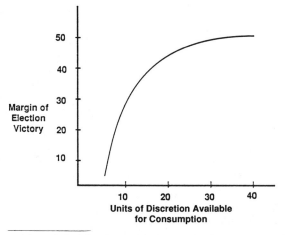

Fig. 2. The relationship between electoral safety and discretion

pendable level of support—a following. Even if constituents never avail themselves of the services supplied by the incumbent, the reliability of the incumbent's services motivates electoral support, especially since the advertised message is not only that "nobody does it better" but also that "nobody else will do it at all."

The theoretical relationship between electoral safety and discretion is shown in figure 2. It can be inferred from the curve that electoral safety increases the amount of discretion a member of Congress is able to exercise or consume. This curve corresponds to the common income-consumption curve that is basic to economic theories of consumer behavior: as income increases (electoral safety), the amount of a good consumed (discretion) also increases. However, the exercise of discretion has its limits, and when reelection margins shrink, discretion is reduced. The exercise of too much discretion may even motivate electoral challenges by those who highlight the incumbent's exercise of discretion and promise to do less of it themselves. For instance, even though no single, unpopular vote by an incumbent would create much of an electoral problem, a string of votes disapproved of by important elements of the incumbent's constituency might. As one legislator told John Kingdon: "I don't think this one vote will be decisive. But I have a string of them. There are several votes where I'm supporting the administration that are unpopular back home. If I were my next opponent, I could put it together and mount a terrific campaign against me" (1973, 42). While such challenges are rarely successful, due to existing barriers of entry, they reduce the cushion of votes that incumbents can afford to lose and still safely win reelection. This reduces discretionary spending by incumbents.

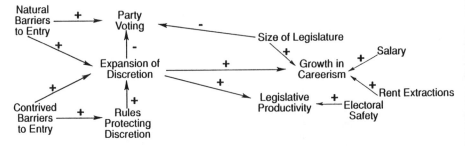

Fig. 3. The role of discretion in the making of Congress. Plus indicates a positive relationship; minus indicates a negative relationship.

Discretion and the Making of Congress

In figure 3 the basic linkages examined in this study are depicted. I view discretion and its expansion as central to the development of Congress—promoting careerism and legislative productivity, as well as accounting for other institutional features. Discretion is hypothesized to respond to the vote surpluses generated by the raising of natural and contrived barriers to entry. Although not analyzed in this study, contrived barriers to entry promote the enactment of laws or rules that protect the discretion of legislators; once enacted, discretion expands. The expansion of discretion, in turn, reduces levels of party voting, as individual legislators become political entrepreneurs rather than party soldiers. The expansion of discretion also produces some positive benefits for Congress: increases in legislative productivity and the attractiveness of a congressional career. The model includes some other variables that have played prominent roles in the development of economic theory: size of legislatures, monetary rewards such as salary, and rent extractions.

The size of legislatures is relevant to the study of Congress for at least two reasons. First, the collective nature of the legislative process and the team-production nature of policy formation make legislature size quite important: the larger the legislature, the greater the transaction costs involved in passing legislation. Simply put, more legislators are involved in decisions, and the costs of reaching those decisions are higher, in larger rather than smaller legislative bodies (Buchanan and Tullock 1962). Second, the larger the legislature, the more difficult the task of monitoring the behavior of legislators; similarly, the larger the legislature, the greater the likelihood of shirking and free riders (members who reap the benefits of passing legislation without contributing in any significant way to the provision of the good). As a result, we can expect the size of the legislature to diminish party voting and legislative productivity but to enhance the attractiveness of a congressional career.

Monetary rewards are an essential element of economic theory, and we can expect such rewards to shape congressional behavior. Specifically, salary increases should enhance the attractiveness of Congress and therefore increase tenure. That is, as salaries have risen, so have the incentives for members to stay in Congress and establish long careers of legislative service. Likewise, the ability of members to profit from doing favors for constituents and aiding in the passage of legislation favorable to groups (rent extractions) should increase the attractiveness of a congressional career.

Conclusion

A major theme in this study is that the expansion of discretion in Congress is inextricably linked to several historical trends that have shaped the modern House. Acting as cause, intervening mechanism, or behavioral consequence, the expansion of discretion is related to the growth in personal contact between legislators and voters, electoral safety of incumbents, terms of congressional service, and the productivity of Congress. It is also associated with declines in party voting and the power of central leaders. There are other relationships among and between these variables that I describe in the chapters that follow.

CHAPTER 2

Discretion-Maximizing Behavior in Congress

Discretionary behavior may take a number of forms, such as displays of altruism in legislative voting (Kalt and Zupan 1984), ideological behavior (Kau and Rubin 1979), shirking, or plain plunder. The costs involved in policing the behavior of legislators reduce the incentives for citizens and party leaders to monitor the actions of legislators, and the more obscure those actions are from public scrutiny, the more discretion legislators exercise. In the sense used in this study, legislators maximize their discretion by keeping their actions as free as possible from constraints imposed by party leaders and constituents. Discretion, like reelection, is a proximate goal—a "goal that must be achieved if other ends are to be entertained" (Mayhew 1974a, 16). Only when legislators feel free to pursue their personal agendas, without fear of voter reprisal or leadership interference, can they entertain the pursuit of more specific goals like power and ideological causes. Legislators, in short, want to give free rein to their own preferences and predilections. The pursuit of power, moral and ideological causes, money, leisure, and even altruism reflects the exercise of discretion by members of Congress. What might appear to be conceptual confusion in defining discretion only reflects the multiple and varied benefits that legislators derive from discretion. This is why discretion has such universal appeal to legislators.

Evidence of Discretion in Congress

There is considerable evidence of discretion being practiced in Congress. I focus in this section on two expressions of the exercise of discretion in Congress: the independence and individuality of legislators in making policy decisions and the tendency for legislators to be above the law. Legislative outcomes often reflect the efforts of dozens of members of Congress pursuing some individual objective, rather than the results of cohesive and coordinated partisan majorities, and most of the policy-making behavior of members involves personal pursuits. Members operate as policy entrepreneurs in a variety of ways: casting votes, drafting bills and amendments, sponsoring legislative measures, participating in floor and committee debates, and engaging in committee and subcommittee deliberations (hearings, markups, investigations, preparations of reports accompanying legislation). Obviously, a member cannot be involved in each and every activity, nor can he or she perform all of the necessary work involved in each task. Congress has helped to alleviate this problem by instituting services such as the Congressional Research Service, Office of Technology Assessment, Congressional Budget Office, and General Accounting Office and expanded committee and personal staff to keep members abreast of legislative actions and to aid in developing legislation. The member orchestrates the interplay of these resources by setting objectives and deciding areas of personal or political interest and the policy alternatives that should be embodied into law. Frequently, legislative recommendations by presidents and party leaders are accepted or rejected by the member depending upon the extent to which the solutions are consistent with his or her goals and attitudes.

Members generally promote policy issues on a unilateral basis. That is, they formulate their legislative measures without much attention to the legislative efforts or initiatives of their colleagues or party leaders. The large number of nearly identical bills introduced each year are expressions of this unilateral promotion of legislative issues. While some duplication of effort can be attributed to the members' desire to gain visibility or to demonstrate legislative effort, an equally relevant explanation is the inclination (if not the preference) of members for a unilateral approach to most issues.

This penchant to ply policy-entrepreneurial talents within the legislative arena often runs counter to the designs of party leaders. "Too many leaders can spoil the policy," might be the refrain that is most frequently voiced by legislative leaders who correctly perceive that members pursue disjointed policies (unconnected policy outcomes) in the absence of centralized sources for coordinating policies. The weaknesses of party leaders (see chapter 3) inhibit their ability to provide direction and to encourage party loyalty. In fact, leaders often find it necessary to tolerate the individualistic policy pursuits of their members in the hope of building support for current or future party policies.

The caricatures of leaders pressuring members and twisting arms to gain votes are outdated. New leadership strategies permit members greater involvement in the formation of party policy (Sinclair 1983). Further, recalcitrant members are not usually punished for failing to support party leaders, and leaders themselves seem willing to accept most excuses for party defections. Pleas of "moral hazard," for example, are rarely questioned or challenged by party leaders. Leaders are more willing to bargain and compromise with their colleagues over policies of interest to the party; persuasion has replaced command as the operative mode for conducting leader-followers relations in the present-day Congress.

Members of Congress also exhibit their discretion in policy-making through their roll call voting. The extent to which members vote based on their own attitudes and beliefs, rather than constituency opinion or the party line, might go unnoticed given the significance of party and constituency in legislative decision making (see, for instance, Clausen 1973). Many studies have found that political parties exercise a profound influence on the voting behavior of members, with the impact of constituency opinion not far behind. That members express their discretion in floor voting is often ignored in accounting for their behavior, but there is substantial evidence that the individual member is, even if overlooked, a significant variable. For instance, Warren Miller and Donald Stokes demonstrate that representatives express their own attitudes and perceptions in roll call voting: the "evidence shows that the Representative's roll call behavior is strongly influenced by his own policy preferences and by his perception of preferences held by the constituency" (1963, 56).

Researchers of legislative turnover and voting behavior generally reach the same conclusion about the influence of individual attitudes in congressional decision making: new members promote policy changes because they exhibit voting patterns that differ from their predecessors (Brady and Lynn 1973; Asher and Weisberg 1978). Thus, replacing one representative with another makes a difference both to parties and to constituents since different policy perspectives are likely to result from such a change. This fact is also evident in Lewis Froman's novel study (1963) of House votes on reciprocal trade issues between 1948 and 1958.

Froman reasoned that if representatives' own attitudes influenced their votes, apart from the effects of party and constituency, representatives replacing incumbents in *one-party districts* (those solidly in the control of one political party or the other) would nevertheless vote differently from the representatives they replaced. He tested this hypothesis and found that those one-party districts that failed to elect the same incumbents during a ten-year period exhibited the greatest shifts over time between support of and opposition to reciprocal trade legislation. Thus, districts that changed representatives experienced a different brand of representation, even though the constituency and party characteristics of the district remained stable!

Perhaps the clearest expression of the impact that members' attitudes can have on their votes is the influence of ideology in House and Senate voting. The common liberal-conservative ideological continuum can account for a substantial proportion of the variation in the voting behavior of members. For example, in separate studies, Keith Poole and R. Steven Daniels (1985) and Herbert Kritzer (1978) found a clear unidimensional organization to major House and Senate votes that reflected a liberal-conservative continuum. There is also evidence that sizable voting blocs on the floor of Congress and in committees (Brady and Bullock 1980; Parker and Parker 1985) organize on the basis of similarities in ideological outlook.

Another expression of legislator demand for leeway in Washington (discretion) is the preference of members for a trustee perspective on their legislative responsibilities. Trustees tend to see their representational obligations as requiring them to exercise their own best judgment in deciding legislative policy; delegates, on the other hand, see their responsibilities as requiring them to follow the dictates of their constituents, rather than their own consciences, in casting roll call votes. Practicality aside, most constituents prescribe the delegate role for their representative (Parker 1986). Members of Congress, however, seem to prefer the more independent position associated with the trustee role: more than 60 percent of the members interviewed in 1977 believed that they should follow their own consciences rather than the dictates of their constituents when the two clash (U.S. Congress, House 1977b).

The trustee role is, of course, a general orientation toward legislative responsibilities, and particular issues or votes may stimulate members to assume delegate roles no matter how committed they are to exercising their own independence. Unusually controversial votes where constituents' sentiment is intense may provide just the type of conditions that quickly turn diehard trustees into delegates. Such conditions aside, members seem to envision their legislative responsibilities as requiring them to exercise their own discretion, giving free rein to the influence of their own attitudes, values, beliefs, and perceptions in making policy decisions.

A final expression of discretion is Congress's practice of excluding itself from coverage of laws that usually apply to everyone else. There is something of a congressional tradition that allows members to live above or outside the law. For instance, Congress has an enormous work force, numbering in the tens of thousands, yet several of the rights granted workers in the private sector and the executive branch—health and safety protections, collective bargaining rights, antidiscrimination guarantees—are denied many of its own employees. Executive branch agencies, including the Central Intelligence Agency and the Federal Bureau of Investigation, have opened many of their files to the public. This step was not a voluntary one: it was forced by Congress through the passage of the Freedom of Information Act. The bill spelled out some exemptions and, not surprisingly, they included Congress, even though Congress, in carrying out the public's business, amasses countless records. The following is a list of some of the major laws that Congress has excluded itself from coverage:

> *Civil Rights Act of 1964* and the *Equal Employment Opportunity Act of 1972* (prohibits discrimination in employment).
> *Equal Pay Act* (requires that women receive the same wages as men for comparable work).
> *Fair Labor Standards Act* (provides minimum wage, overtime, and child-labor protections).

National Labor Relations Act (requires employees to recognize and bargain collectively with unions that have won the right to represent employees).

Occupational Safety and Health Act (requires employers to meet safety and health standards in their workplaces).

Social Security Act (taxes employers and employees to finance the social security trust funds).

Freedom of Information Act (gives the public the right to examine most records kept by federal agencies).

Privacy Act (requires government agencies to ensure the confidentiality of the files they maintain on individuals).

How Members of Congress Maximize Discretion

The major assumption in my model is that legislators act as if they were trying to maximize discretion, but where is the best place to exercise discretion? There is no scarcity of places for legislators to exercise discretion, but there are several reasons why discretion-maximizing legislators might turn to congressional committees to practice discretion:

1. The smaller size of congressional committees and ruling majorities relative to the entire legislature maximizes the influence of individual members—a higher payoff to the practice of discretion.
2. Committee decisions are normally less public (visible) than decisions made on the floor of the legislature; hence, committees provide good opportunities to exercise discretion and escape detection by constituents, groups, and even party leaders.
3. Committees traffic in particularized benefits, providing considerable opportunity to extract rents and other extralegislative benefits from groups and favor buyers (Niskanan 1971; Mayhew 1974a; Fiorina 1977).
4. Committee assignments are protected against the discretionary actions of party leaders (i.e., seniority system).

There are two major ways in which legislators can maximize their discretion in committees: increase the range of discretion already practiced within committees, such as increased levels of ideological or altruistic voting, or increase the opportunities to exercise discretion by expanding their areas of discretion. It is extremely hard to detect, in an unobtrusive manner, the first type of discretion-maximization. The extent to which legislators expand their areas of discretion can be identified, however, by observing increases in the number of committee assignments held by legislators: given the monopoly exercised by committees over the legislative agenda, increases in committee assignments expand the areas in which legislators can exercise discretion. Simply put, the expansion of committee assignments is the type of behavior we would expect of legislators bent upon maximizing discretion.[1]

It might be suggested that as members are added to individual committees, existing committee members will find their investments in the committee system devalued or depreciated because each member's share of committee power must now be shared with more committee members. Despite this disadvantage to the expansion of committee seats, most members gain from such an expansion since they are able to diversify their portfolios of investments, gaining access to other areas of the legislative agenda; this enables legislators to participate in more legislative deals and to be able to offer more "services" (influence over a greater diversity of legislation and regulations) to groups, constituents, presidents, party leaders, and other legislators.

In the model, the committee system subdivides the agenda into smaller areas and grants each committee exclusive rights to produce legislation in that area. The system benefits individual committee members because, while they give up nonexclusive access to a large portion of the agenda, they gain exclusive control over a limited part of it. One factor that makes committee decision making an attractive channel for the exercise of discretion is the element of agenda control that is inherent in committee decisions. Because the legislature as a whole does not shape the bills that emerge from committee, the committee is in a position to place the legislature on its all-or-nothing demand curve (Niskanan 1971).[2] The only constraint on each committee is that legislation must be approved by the whole body to become effective.

Legislatures can, of course, modify a committee's product by amending its legislation on the floor, but most successful amendments are sponsored by

---

1. One example of the expression of legislator discretion is the independence of members in casting votes in Congress (see Parker 1989). Some of this independence is represented by the ideological nature of roll call voting. While political scientists seem fairly comfortable with the notion of ideological voting (for an exception, see Clausen 1973), others are not, and the controversy is not even close to a resolution within economics.

Some economists (Kalt and Zupan 1984, for example) have sought to measure such independence in terms of the variation in voting that is left unexplained after the introduction of variables measuring the characteristics of constituencies. Other economists (Peltzman 1985) contend that this residual only reflects the imperfect measurement of constituency attributes, primarily economic ones. While most social scientists would be sympathetic toward attempts to measure ideology in legislative voting, using error terms—residuals—to measure this concept is fraught with problems. Rather than continuing the debate over what the residuals mean, or their systematic properties, more effort needs to be directed toward identifying *other* indicators of legislator independence. The expansion of committee assignments, as analyzed in this inquiry, is offered as an alternative indicator of legislator independence.

2. Niskanan and others (Shepsle and Weingast 1987; Weingast and Marshall 1988) contend that committees are composed of preference outliers (i.e., committee members whose preferences differ from those of the larger legislature). For some effective counterarguments, see Krehbiel 1990.

members who are in a committee minority but share the views supported by a majority of the full legislature. Even here, then, committee membership looms important in how legislation is shaped on the floor of the legislature. For example, Steven Smith (1986) notes that from 1955 to 1980 about half of the amendments in the House of Representatives were proposed by committee members even though committee members make up substantially less than half of the House. Even more telling, the success rate for amendments was 60 percent when proposed by committee members but only 44 percent when proposed by those outside the committees.

Further, requiring amendments to bills to be germane, as in the House of Representatives, reduces the influence of noncommittee members: they normally lack the policy expertise required to amend specialized legislation, and they are prohibited from injecting unrelated matters into the policy decisions made by the entire legislature. This requirement protects the committee's right to its portion of the agenda. Indeed, Kenneth Shepsle and Barry Weingast contend that congressional committees also possess *ex post veto power:*

> Once it has opened the gates and made a proposal and after the legislature has worked its will, either accepting the proposal or modifying it in some germane fashion, the committee now may either sanction the final product or restore the status quo, X^0 [status quo point]. A committee with an ex post veto possesses the power to protect itself against welfare-reducing changes in the status quo. (1987, 93).

Modeling the Expansion of Discretion

In order for discretion to expand, barriers to entry must reduce electoral competition. There is considerable evidence that competition for congressional offices has in fact diminished: the supply of competitive candidates has declined, and the electoral safety of incumbents has increased (Fiorina 1977; Garand and Gross 1984; Calvert and Ferejohn 1983; Parker 1986; Alford and Brady 1988). In figure 4 the trend in the electoral safety of incumbents is illustrated.[3] From the Forty-seventh (1881–82) to the Fifty-seventh (1901–2) Congresses, one-third or more of all contested elections could be classified as marginal (incumbents' vote percentages in the 45–55 percent range). After the turn of the century, from the Fifty-ninth (1905–6) Congress until the Eighty-ninth (1965–66) Congress, the vast majority of House elections resulted in less than one-third marginal elections in districts. The 1920s were a particu-

---

3. The data on incumbents' election marginality are drawn from the work of John Alford and David Brady 1989: they exclude reapportionment elections—those immediately following a reapportionment—because these elections distort levels of incumbents' electoral vulnerability in the time series. They define marginally elected incumbents as those who have received between 45 and 55 percent of the district vote.

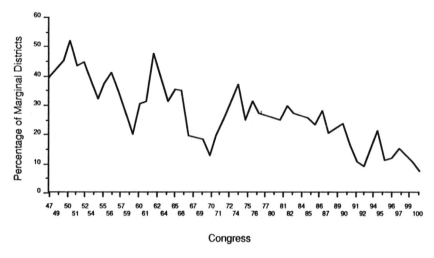

Fig. 4. Percentage of marginal districts in House elections, 1880–1988 (45–55 percent of the vote). Excludes the congressional election following each decennial reapportionment.

larly distinctive period in the history of electoral safety in the House: the 1926 election, for instance, produced a level of electoral safety (14 percent) that was not exceeded until 1968, when the proportion of marginal elections declined to 11.7 percent. The decline in marginal elections accelerated further after the Eighty-ninth Congress, with only one election (in 1974) having more than 20 percent of the incumbents' victories falling in the marginal category. In general, electoral marginality was relatively stable in the 25–30 percent range between 1946 and 1964; however, it has dropped to the low teens since the late 1960s.[4] In the 1986 and 1988 elections, less than 10 percent of the incumbents' elections could be classified as marginal. The trend toward greater electoral safety suggests that barriers to entry have been raised even higher during recent decades.

Measuring Barriers to Entry

To measure barriers to entry, I examine two types of barriers: electoral realignments and incumbent advertising. As noted earlier, electoral realignments

---

4. For a good summary of the literature dealing with the decline in competition in House elections, see Fiorina 1977. Other evidence of the increased safety of incumbents can be found in Mayhew 1974b, Calvert and Ferejohn 1983, Alford and Brady 1988, Parker 1986, and Garand and Gross 1984.

have characteristically induced electoral safety for long periods of time (Brady 1988). My measure of the influence of realignments is the number of years since the last realignment (i.e., 1860, 1896, 1932). While the effects of realignments eventually decay to the point of diminishing previous levels of electoral safety (Brady 1988), the modeling of this aspect of the dynamics of realignments fails to improve upon the simpler (transformed) linear relationship between the length of a realignment and increased electoral safety and discretion. For these reasons, I have restricted the analysis to the simple linear effects of the length of a realignment period as a barrier to entry that reduces electoral competition and promotes the expansion of discretion.

It is difficult, it not impossible, to obtain a historical measure of incumbent advertising. For one thing, figures on such relevant indicators of advertising as mass mailings do not span much legislative history;[5] more importantly, there is no historical record of the types of messages disseminated by legislators or their frequency. In the absence of a more explicit measure of the advertising activity of legislators, I use the scheduled days of recess for each Congress.[6] This measure is a relevant indicator of congressional advertising for two reasons. First, members spend recesses *in their districts* by and large: each day of recess translates into a day spent in the district and an opportunity for personal advertising (Parker 1986). Second, recess periods reflect government subsidies for advertising since legislators are paid while visiting their districts and the costs of these visits are subsidized by the government. Therefore, recesses can be viewed as government-subsidized opportunities for legislators to meet with past, present, and future customers for their services and to generate business (i.e., increase demand).

The trend in the proportion of the legislative session devoted to recesses rose over time (fig. 5). Between the Fifty-sixth (1899–1900) and Sixtieth (1907–8) Congresses, the ratio of days of recess to days in session increased, before declining to pre-1900 levels. The ratio rose again for a brief period between the Sixty-eighth (1923–24) and Seventy-first (1929–30) Congresses before reaching the lowest levels in the entire series—the Seventy-second (1931–32) to Seventy-seventh (1941–42) Congresses. Another relatively high ratio of recess days occurred between the Seventy-eighth (1943–44) and Eighty-second (1951–52) Congresses. Recess days rose in an almost monotonic fashion after the Eighty-ninth (1965–66) Congress, increasing steadily from more than a 1:4 ratio of recess days to actual days in legislative session

---

5. The number of years for which data are available suggest that mass mailings have indeed increased over time. See, for instance, Cover 1977 and Ornstein, Mann, and Malbin 1990, 164, for relevant data on mass mailings.

6. These data are drawn from U.S. Congress, *Congressional Directory* 1965–87, vols. 89–100.

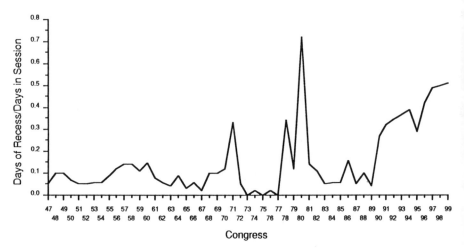

Fig. 5. The ratio of days of recess to actual days in session

to a 1:2 ratio in the Ninety-eighth (1983–84) and Ninety-ninth (1985–86) Congresses. Clearly, incumbent advertising has increased over time.

I have measured the influence of advertising as the ratio of days of recess to legislative days (i.e., days in session minus days of recess). The change in product advertising that occurred during the mid-1960s (an emphasis on personal contact) suggests a possible interaction effect between incumbent advertising and the expansion of discretion. Specifically, after 1965, days of recess should have had an even greater effect on increasing discretion than in earlier periods because the resources for enhancing legislator-constituent contact were also growing (table 1).

Personal contact not only enhances the demand for constituency service but it also promotes confidence in the member of Congress (Parker and Parker 1989). A member's level of trust among his or her constituents influences how much discretion the member can safely exercise in Washington without stirring voters to revolt:

> He [the legislator] cultivates home support not just because he wants to be reelected. He cultivates support at home, also, because he wants voting (and other) leeway in Washington. . . . Political support at home guarantees the congressman some freedom to maneuver on Capitol Hill. (Fenno 1978, 157)

I represent incumbent advertising, and the change in that advertising, with the following expression:

$$A + CA,$$

where

A = level of incumbent advertising (ratio of days of recess to days in session) and

C = one for all Congresses after the Eighty-eighth, and zero otherwise.

The latter term, CA, is designed to capture the change in home styles (Fenno 1978)—product advertising—that began in 1965 (Parker 1986). The estimate associated with A measures the impact of incumbent advertising, while the estimate associated with the term CA measures the effects of the change in incumbent advertising after 1965. In sum, incumbent advertising, the change in incumbent advertising, and the length of realignment periods should create barriers to entry that motivate legislators to expand their existing levels of discretion.

I have assumed that electoral realignments create barriers to entry by reducing competition; and that additional declines in electoral competition reflect the increased personal advertising of constituency services. There is some empirical support for these positions since all three of these variables are correlated with declines in competition in House elections. The percentage of marginal districts in House elections between 1881 and 1988 is negatively related to length of a realignment ($r = -.46$), the ratio of recess days to days in session ($r = -.54$), and the post-1965 change in advertising ($r = -.62$).

Rules Protecting Discretion

There are two basic types of rules that protect the discretion of legislators: informal norms and formal rules. Foremost in the category of informal norms is seniority, a norm that is rarely violated. Still, seniority is only a norm and lacks the *durability* and force of law; therefore, it is more subject to violation. This suggests that formal rules, like legislative acts, may be more important in increasing discretion than informal rules, like seniority, because of the durability of formal rules. (For an insightful analysis of the relevance of the durability of laws to the behavior of legislators, see Landes and Posner 1975.) Two formal legislative acts that increased the discretion of legislators were the Legislative Reorganization Act of 1946 and the Legislative Reorganization Act of 1970.

Among its many provisions, the 1946 act required committee chairs to report promptly any measure approved by their committees to the House, and it prohibited chairs from reporting measures to the floor unless a majority of members were present for the deliberations. The 1946 act also "expanded the range of policy areas controlled by many committees" by reducing the number of committees and consolidating jurisdictions (Kravitz 1990, 376); this increased the attractiveness of committees as places to practice discretion. The 1970 act constrained committee chairs even further, requiring committees to have written rules and restricting the use of proxy voting—a check on the arbitrary use of power by chairpersons; other features included allowing a committee majority to call a meeting when the chair refused to do so and guaranteeing that a majority of minority members on a committee would be allowed to call witnesses during hearings.

These two legislative acts share a number of common features, but the most significant from the perspective of this study is that both acts restricted the power of leaders—party and committee leaders. The 1946 act increased the autonomy of the House committee system (Davidson 1990), thereby reducing the power of centralized party leaders. But even an autonomous committee has little value if the independence of the committee does not translate into discretion for committee members. As long as committee chairs retain autocratic control over their committees, the ability of members to exercise discretion is severely constrained. Before the onset of the 1970 reforms, committee leaders exercised considerable influence over committee outcomes. The 1970 reforms, by restricting the influence of committee leaders, reduced the constraints on legislators and encouraged them to expand their existing levels of discretion. In combination with the 1946 act, committee members gained rights to exercise discretion within an autonomous committee system.

I have measured the effects of rules protecting discretion with two dummy variables to capture the impact of the 1946 and 1970 legislative reorganization acts, coding each Congress following the adoption of these legislative acts with a one and assigning a zero to all other Congresses, and one variable measuring the number of uncompensated violations of seniority in the selection of House committee chairs.[7] Violations in the seniority rule in selecting committee chairs reduce members' investments in their assignments by increasing uncertainty about the security of committee investments. The result is a reduction in the level of discretion exercised.

Expansion of Discretion

The expansion of discretion is measured by the increased investment of members in committee assignments: the mean number of committee assignments

---

7. Seniority violations between the Forty-seventh and Eighty-eighth Congresses are drawn from Polsby, Gallaher, and Rundquist 1969; seniority violations from the Eighty-ninth through the One hundredth Congress are calculated from U.S. Congress, *Congressional Directory* 1881–1987, vols. 47–100.

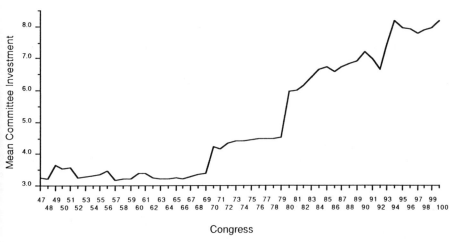

Fig. 6. The growth in committee assignments relative to the size of the committee system. Mean Committee Investment indicates the mean number of committee assignments divided by the number of standing committees.

relative to the number of committees in the House (U.S. Congress, *Congressional Directory* 1881–1987, vols. 47–100). Figure 6 traces the growth in committee assignments per House member. Distinct transitions appear around the Seventieth (1927–28), Eightieth (1947–48), and Ninety-fourth (1975–76) Congresses, producing significant leaps in the mean number of committee assignments in the House of Representatives. The expansion of committee assignments should respond to (1) the establishment of rules protecting the discretion and independence of committee members and (2) the strength of barriers to entry. The greater the protections, and the more restrictive the barriers, the more discretion expands (i.e., committee assignments increase). In short, as a realignment continues, and as the ratio of recess days to actual days in session increases, committee assignments grow and discretion expands. In addition, the reduction in seniority violations and the enactment of the 1946 and 1970 legislative reorganization acts should also increase the exercise of discretion.

These relationships can be specified in the following manner:

$$D = f(E, A, CA, S, R_1, R_2),$$

where

D = expansion of discretion (mean number of committee assignments relative to the number of committees),

E = length of electoral realignment (years since the last realignment— 1860, 1896, and 1932),

A = level of incumbent advertising (ratio of days of recess to days in session),

C = one for all Congresses after the Eighty-eighth, and zero otherwise (CA represents a change in advertising—an emphasis on *personal* contact with constituents),

S = seniority violations (number of uncompensated violations of seniority in the House),

R_1 = Legislative Reorganization Act of 1946 (one for all Congresses after 1946, and zero otherwise), and

R_2 = Legislative Reorganization Act of 1970 (one for all Congresses after 1970, and zero otherwise).

Findings

The estimates associated with the above equation are presented in table 2. It is clear from this table that the two legislative reorganizations (1946 and 1970) significantly increased the exercise of discretion by encouraging the expansion of committee assignments; the 1946 reorganization had the greatest impact on the expansion of discretion ($B = .57$). Both measures of incumbent advertising also produce significant positive relationships: incumbent advertising ($B = .13$) and the change in advertising ($B = .14$) created by home-style changes commencing in the mid-1960s have increased discretion *independently*. There does not, however, appear to be significant relationships between discretion and either uncompensated violations of seniority (eq. 1 and eq. 2) or the length of realignment periods (eq. 1). In short, legislative reorganization plans and contrived barriers to entry—incumbent advertising—are the only significant influences on the expansion of discretion; together they account for 97 percent of the variation in the expansion of discretion (eq. 3), and these estimates are not significantly biased by autocorrelation (not significant at .05 level).

Because of the Democratic reforms during the mid-1970s that made the selection of committee chairs subject to a vote, less importance may be attributed to seniority violations today than in the past. Perhaps a more sensitive measure, such as the percentage of time that committee majorities are ignored by party and/or committee leaders, would yield more positive results regarding the influence of informal norms. Different calculations of uncompensated seniority violations (e.g., the percentage of violations rather than the absolute number) proved even less reliable than the calculations presented here. Despite these negative findings, it would be unwise to discount the effects of informal rules in expanding discretion.

TABLE 2. Explaining the Expansion of Discretion in the House of
Representatives (Standardized Regression Coefficients)

Variables	Eq. 1	Eq. 2	Eq. 3
1946 Legislative Reorganization Act	.560*	.570*	.57*
	(12.340)[a]	(14.100)	(14.26)
1970 Legislative Reorganization Act	.320*	.310*	.31*
	(7.790)	(7.890)	(8.97)
Change in product advertising	.140*	.140*	.14*
	(3.100)	(3.150)	(3.20)
Incumbent advertising	.130*	.130*	.13*
	(3.190)	(3.380)	(3.43)
Seniority violations	−.010	−.000	
	(−.148)	(−.024)	
Number of years since the last			
realignment[b]	.020		
	(.615)		
Statistics:			
Multiple R^2	.990	.990	.99
R^2	.970	.970	.97
Adjusted R^2	.970	.970	.97
N	54	54	54
Durbin-Watson statistic	1.740[d]	1.720[d]	1.72[c]

[a] T-values are shown in parentheses.
[b] A natural logarithmic transformation has been applied to this variable.
[c] Not significant at .05 level.
[d] Not significant at .01 level.
* Statistically significant at .01 level.

Conclusion

In conclusion, there is evidence that contrived barriers to entry, produced
through government-subsidized advertising, and the enactment of rules protecting the discretion of members of Congress motivated incumbents to expand existing levels of discretion. As a result, legislators began to acquire
more committee assignments and gain greater access to the legislative agenda.
If access to the legislative agenda translates into more policy areas to ply one's
legislative skills and interests, then legislators have increased their areas of
political influence. Their access to power expanded in a very real sense.[8]

---

8. Additional rule changes, some adopted by House Democrats in 1973, restricted the
power of committee chairs even more. Because these latter rules may not benefit members of the
two parties equally, and are not part of the formal House rules, and since the timing of these
Democratic reforms is so close to the 1970 reorganization, I did not include a measure of these
specific party rules in the model. From the perspective of this study, such reforms are considered
less durable than the legislative acts examined in the statistical analysis.

The expansion of committee assignments may generate additional rent extractions, foreign junkets, and/or opportunities for policy-making influence. In each case, the added assignments may produce more money, leisure, or political power. Therefore, it cannot be concluded that the expansion of committee assignments only reflects the accrual of policy influence. However, it is the policy influence component of discretion, rather than the monetary element, that is the most valuable to legislators (see chap. 4).

CHAPTER 3

Partisanship and Productivity

Like Congress, the role of party leaders has changed over time. They are no longer the commanders of cohesive party majorities; today's party leaders are far more dependent upon the willingness of legislators to follow their lead than on their ability to demand party allegiance. Simply put, there are not many incentives for following, and too few disincentives for opposing, the wishes and preferences of party leaders. This makes the task of leadership all that more difficult for party leaders in a discretion-maximizing legislature.

Why Party Leaders Can't Demand Loyalty

If the powers of present legislative leaders are compared to those possessed by past party leaders, it is clear that present-day leaders operate at a distinct disadvantage. Barbara Sinclair succinctly characterizes the legislative plight faced by most party leaders in the twentieth century:

> The current leaders lack both a strong intraparty policy consensus and resources sufficient to affect decisively members' goal attainment. They cannot count on members' goal directed behavior being conducive to party maintenance or coalition-building success; nor can they assure desirable member behavior by use of rewards and punishments. (1983, 238)

Near the turn of the century, however, party leaders were in a far better position to influence the goal attainment of their members, and the legislative agenda in Congress. The powerful Speakers of the House who served during this period epitomize the strong party leaders of the past—leaders who were not the least bit timid about exploiting their powers to affect legislative outcomes.

Committee assignments are prized possessions for most members, and past House Speakers have exercised unusual influence over them.

Those who desired a change in assignment knew full well that their chances of advancement depended on the good graces of the Speaker.

> Conversely, since in this age seniority was far from sacrosanct as it is today, members were also aware that to alienate the Speaker was to risk loss of a chairmanship, an assignment, or rank on a committee. (Cooper and Brady 1981, 412)

During this period, then, to oppose the Speaker was to risk what members cherished most—projects and policies important to constituents (and therefore reelection) and committee assignments that provided avenues for realizing personal legislative goals.

The reduction in the formal powers of the Speaker between 1909 and 1911 had the expected effect of heightening the power and independence of individual members and organizational units, such as congressional committees, and facilitating expressions of party factionalism. By 1940, the power of party leadership in the House had been altered significantly by placing a more severe set of constraints on these leaders than in 1910. Party leaders were forced to engage in the laborious and painful process of organizing shifting majorities behind specific legislation by *negotiating* with members for their votes and by *bargaining* with committees and their chairs to gain their cooperation and support:

> Denied the power they possessed over the individual member under Czar rule, party leaders began to function less as the commanders of a stable party majority and more as brokers trying to assemble particular majorities behind particular bills. Denied the power they possessed over the organizational structure under Czar rule or caucus rule, party leaders began to function less as directors of the organizational units and more as bargainers for their support. (Cooper and Brady 1981, 417)

As a result, party leaders made considerably more use of their own personal political skills to encourage party discipline rather than their now limited sources of institutional power.

Because of the effectiveness of the rewards and sanctions possessed by past legislative leaders, members had little choice except to follow their party leaders; to do otherwise was not even a viable alternative since past leaders possessed the type of resources that made legislative life worthwhile (or hell) for many members. This factor alone probably made the arguments and pleas of party leaders quite effective with their members. As party leaders have, of necessity, come to depend almost entirely on personal skills for mobilizing party support behind legislation, the compulsion to follow party leaders "or else" has also eased.

There is very little systematic evidence of the extent to which party leaders depend upon personal persuasion or pressure in their dealings with other members. One estimate of the reliance of party leaders on personal skills of persuasion is provided by Randall Ripley's study (1967) of party leadership in the House of Representatives. A particularly interesting aspect of his study dealt with the role of party leaders. Ripley asked a sample of sixty members during the Eighty-eighth Congress (1963–64) to describe the kinds of appeals that party leaders used to achieve party unity. As a result of these interviews, Ripley identified four categories of appeals: personal ("I need you" or "the President needs your support"), party (loyalty to party or to its legislative program), merits of the issue (arguments dealing with the substance or impact of the legislation), and pressure (implicit rewards or punishments).

As we would expect given the emphasis of present-day party leaders on persuasion and bargaining in their dealings with colleagues, the largest category of leadership appeals is personal: 86 percent of the Democrats and 48 percent of the Republicans interviewed mentioned personal appeals in describing the efforts of party leaders to elicit their support. Less than one-quarter of the members mentioned pressure in the form of implicit rewards or sanctions—23 percent of the Democrats and 12 percent of the Republicans (Ripley 1967, 146).

When pressure is applied, it is normally focused on the most recalcitrant elements of the party; hence, most members escape punishment not because they are necessarily strong adherents to the party's cause, but because party leaders prefer to subject only the most offensive members to pressure. Thus, Ripley found that Southern Democrats and Northeastern Republicans— groups historically at odds with their parties' leaders—were more likely than other legislators to associate the appeals of party leaders with pressure: 36 percent of the Southern Democrats and 22 percent of the Northeastern Republicans mentioned rewards and punishments in describing how their leaders appealed to them for support (1967, 147).

Perhaps a more pertinent question regarding the efficacy of the resources possessed by present party leaders is their effectiveness in promoting party support. Again, Ripley's interviews with House members can shed some light on this question. When asked, "What can the leadership do to you to if you do not support their position?" members gave four basic responses: nothing (leaders have no leverage over members who refuse to go along with the party), isolation (psychological pressure), projects involving funds for constituents or small pieces of general legislation could be affected, and committee assignments might be withheld or opposed. The impoverished state of present House leaders is evident by the fact that more than one-third of those interviewed reported that their leaders were relatively powerless and could not exercise significant leverage over them (Ripley 1967)!

One reason why members who oppose their parties are free to do so is because party leaders are apprehensive about punishing members in any way.

In short, party leaders are reluctant to crack the whip to induce party support. Not only do most party leaders prefer the carrot to the stick, but they abhor using the stick at all. Part of the reason for the resistance to negative sanctions is that so few exist, but equally important is the fact that negative pressure may severely damage tomorrow's as well as today's efforts at coalition building. As one legislator observed:

> The theory behind that [resistance to the use of negative sanctions] is not only peace and tranquility and the "polite thing to do" but also "there's always tomorrow"; there's going to be another vote on another issue and you can't stay mad at anybody. If something happens and it doesn't work out, you may get mad momentarily but there's no percentage in staying mad. You need the guy tomorrow. It's a very practical aspect. There's always tomorrow. (Sinclair 1983, 89–90)

In addition to resisting the use of sanctions, party leaders are even unlikely to withhold rewards from those who oppose them. "Withholding favors from such members, the leaders believe, is likely to alienate them rather than produce leadership desired behavior" (Sinclair 1983, 238–39). Thus members correctly perceive their leadership as unlikely to use coercion to promote party unity, and the unwillingness of leaders to withhold favors from those who oppose party policies further weakens the incentives for following the dictates of party leaders.

However, the resources available to present party leaders for affecting legislative outcomes should not be ignored. The powers of the Speaker of the House, for example, to determine the length of recorded votes and to set deadlines for reporting a bill referred to several committees—multiple referrals of legislation—provide the Speaker with strategic vantage points (Sinclair 1983, 35–36). Furthermore, party leaders can help members on an individual basis by occasionally intervening on their behalf in the affairs of other leaders and organizational subunits like committees. An aide to former House Speaker "Tip" O'Neill described the utility of such interventions in these terms:

> "Tip" can't assure it, but he can talk to some people. Now, some of those people he talks to, even his friends on Appropriations, might say, " 'Tip,' you don't want to ask me this; it's a stupid request, you know this thing ought to be cut out." And "Tip" will say, "the guy asked me to ask you." So he really hasn't done anything, maybe it *will* make a difference, and they ask. They want to use his powers, members do, to get things done for their own districts or their amendments on the floor; they ask him all the time. He doesn't always do them; they may think he does. He may be

effective and he may not be when you ask him. But they like him to try. (Sinclair 1983, 38)

Despite these resources, party leaders are ill-equipped to demand any sort of party orthodoxy from their members. Most resources are just insufficient to affect member goals. For instance, party leaders can help members raise campaign funds, and some members may indeed benefit from such efforts, but most incumbents raise more money than they actually need in their campaigns (Goldenberg and Traugott 1984). Furthermore, it is beyond question that party leaders would prefer to see the least-loyal members of the party replaced with more supportive ones; however, party leaders realize that any attempt to withhold electoral support or assistance is only likely to damage the party's position in Congress. If the party deviant is reelected without the help of the party, his or her party loyalty is apt to plummet even further, and if not reelected, his or her replacement is likely to be a member of the opposition party. There is no dilemma here: rarely would a leader prefer a member of the opposition party to the most uncooperative party member.

Other member goals are equally resistant to leadership influence. Norms, for example, limit the discretion of leaders in making committee assignments and in appointing members to offices within the party. "By and large," Sinclair concludes, "the leadership can affect an individual member's goal achievement in only a peripheral or sporadic rather than a central and continuous manner" (1983, 27). The more leaders can facilitate or prevent the realization of goals, the greater their influence over their members; their influence, however, also depends upon their willingness to use whatever resources they have toward this end. The inability of party leaders to significantly influence the attainment of important goals and their resistance to withholding rewards from party defectors testify to the weakness of present party leaders.

The adoption of automatic decision rules has further reduced the power of political leaders to dispense favors and rewards or discipline members. What at one time or another fell firmly within the range of discretion associated with the prerogatives of party leadership has now become a matter of rights. Office resources are automatically given to each member, and beyond the manipulation of party leaders. Appointments to committees have become routinized to the point that most members realize their preferred assignments after very short terms in Congress (Gertzog 1976). Finally, once members are appointed to committees, they may serve on them as long as they like. These automatic decision rules mean that most members in the present Congress can "get along" without "going along," depriving leaders of important leverage over their members.

Party voting is one expression of the capacity of leaders and parties to induce team loyalty. There are a number of ways to define party voting, but

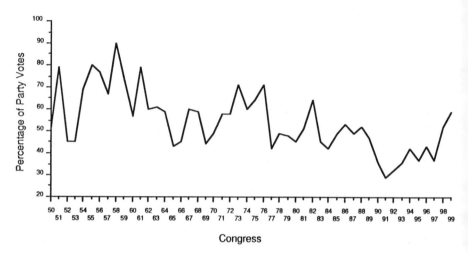

Fig. 7. The percentage of party votes in the House of Representatives

two of the most widely used classify party votes as those in which (1) 90 percent of one party opposed 90 percent of the members of the other party or (2) votes in which 50 percent of one party opposed 50 percent of the members of the other party (fig. 7). With the latter definition, which is obviously less restrictive than the former, party voting in Congress attains a more respectable level. Regardless of one's preference for either of these definitions of party voting, the trend in both reveals the same pattern: a decline in party votes over time.

The trend in party voting since 1887 is illustrated in figure 7. It is clear from this figure that party voting has declined over time, although there is a temporary upsurge very late in the series. Party votes were relatively frequent before 1915, but from the Sixty-fifth Congress (1917–18) to the Ninety-seventh Congress (1981–82), party votes occurred less than 50 percent of the time during the vast majority of the Congresses. Post-1915 highs in party voting occurred between the Seventy-first (1929–30) and Seventy-sixth (1939–40), and the Ninety-eighth (1983–84) and One hundredth Congresses (1987–88). An economic explanation for this trend in party unity focuses on factors that diminish team spirit in team-production situations.

An Economic Perspective on Party Unity

Party cohesion attains high levels following elections where intense differences separate the parties, and party loyalties account for most votes.[1] Such

---

1. For an excellent, noneconomic explanation of the changes in party voting over time, see Brady, Cooper, and Hurley 1979.

elections, frequently described as *critical elections* or *realignments,* produce legislative majorities that are unusually responsive to partisan directives. Unfortunately for most party leaders, realigning elections are anomalies; hence, party leaders cannot rely upon the occurrence of such elections, and the high levels of party loyalty they generate among legislators, as a constant or even intermittent force in mobilizing party members.

A legislature composed of discretion-maximizing incumbents creates even more problems for party leaders since they complicate two of the major functions of leaders: keeping the legislature productive and clearing the market for legislation (making "deals"). If legislators do not live up to their bargains and/or facilitate the production of legislation, the political fortunes of party leaders (and their utility incomes) suffer. In short, if by exercising discretion legislators shirk, the costs to party leaders in producing legislation increase.

High levels of party loyalty or cohesion enable leaders to keep the legislature productive at low levels of cost because the team spirit associated with party loyalty deters shirking. Party leaders, however, cannot depend upon party loyalty to prevent members from shirking: party loyalty—loyalty to the team—might reduce shirking (see Alchian and Demsetz 1972), but the lack of voter loyalties to the parties reduces legislators' loyalties. If voters are not loyal to the parties themselves, they are unlikely to make party loyalty a condition for continuation in office; hence, there is no incentive for legislators to exhibit such loyalty. Party leaders refrain from shirking themselves, and are willing to monitor the behavior of others, because they can claim the surplus benefits obtained by reducing shirking in the production of legislation. Party leaders function like *residual claimants:* the more efficient and effective the legislative efforts of leaders, the greater the returns they receive.[2] To prevent shirking, leaders often resort to "tied sales" (linking access to a specific benefit to a member's contribution to the team, or collective, effort). Earlier and more certain passage of legislation is an example of a tied sale: a reward that leaders pass out to their most-loyal members—those who can be counted upon to keep their bargains (Crain, Leavens, and Tollison 1986).

The returns to party leaders are in the form of "chits" (favors) owed the leaders. Party leaders serve as intermediaries in arranging bargains, and they

---

2. According to Armen A. Alchian and Harold Demsetz 1972, the monitor earns his or her residual by reducing the shirking of team members. In order to reduce shirking the residual claimant must have the power to revise the contract terms and incentives of individual members without having to terminate or alter every other's contract. While each member can terminate his or her own membership on the team, only the residual claimant may unilaterally terminate the membership of any of the other members without terminating the team itself or his or her association with the team; moreover, the residual claimant alone can expand or reduce the membership of the team (e.g., political party) or alter the mix of membership. Alchian and Demsetz also add the right of the claimant to sell these rights.

accumulate chits for arranging the passage of legislation and actually passing that same legislation. Some of these favors, both past and present, are used by party leaders to arrange the exchanges necessary to pass legislation; chits not used in negotiating these agreements can be used at the discretion of party leaders. The accumulated chits owed party leaders enable them to influence policy outcomes far beyond that of the average member and allow them to further personal goals. Therefore, leaders have a strong incentive to make and keep the legislature productive, since the passage of legislation creates the favors that they can spend with discretion. The fewer the chits used in passing legislation, the greater the profit (i.e., favors) leaders earn; hence, party leaders not only want the legislature to be productive but also to be efficient so that fewer favors have to be expended in passing legislation. This provides the rationale for party leaders to monitor the behavior of party members: the leaders are residual claimants to all gains obtained by reducing shirking on the part of others.

As realignments continue, factionalism in the dominant party reduces team spirit (party loyalty) and therefore increases shirking. Not only does the dominant party begin to fragment, but the costs of shirking (to party leaders) increase. Declines in team spirit, resulting from the disappearance of intense realignment-generated partisan majorities, increase monitoring costs for leaders.[3] Increased monitoring costs and increased shirking due to declines in team spirit reduce party voting. The resources of party leaders also are strained to a greater degree when team spirit fails to restrain shirking and the expansion of discretion. The result is that as realignments fade so does the team spirit (and party voting) they initially induce.

Legislators also have greater opportunities to shirk the larger the legislature, simply because the monitoring costs of party leaders expand with the size of the legislature. Here, the logic of collective action also seems particularly relevant to party leaders. One of the forces driving the logic of collective action is that the opportunities for a legislator to become a free rider and shirk his or her responsibility to contribute to the collective or team effort depend on the imperceptibility of the legislator's contribution. In large legislatures, like other large-sized groups, a single legislator's efforts will largely go unnoticed. This creates incentives for legislators to conceal as many of their activities as possible from the scrutiny of party leaders. Once removed from the watchful

---

3. Alchian and Demsetz (1972) suggest that team spirit and loyalty reduce shirking:

> If one could enhance a common interest in nonshirking in the guise of a team loyalty or team spirit, the team would be more efficient. In those sports where team activity is most clearly exemplified, the sense of loyalty and team spirit is most strongly urged. Obviously, the team is better, with team spirit and loyalty, because of the reduced shirking—not because of some other feature inherent in loyalty or spirit as such. (790)

eyes of leaders due to the size of the legislature, party members can exploit their anonymity to shirk.

Party leaders, even when discovering shirking may ignore it because the individual's effort would not alter the outcome of legislation, and future legislative negotiations might be damaged by punishing a recalcitrant party member. For instance, punishing party members may cost party leaders dearly in terms of favors they've collected by acting as intermediaries in legislative deals: a punished member may renege on future and present obligations, or party leaders may have to cash in some favors to turn party members against another. Even rational legislators favoring the punishment of party deviants are unlikely to reveal their true preferences, thereby escalating costs further (i.e., bribes may be necessary to encourage support) and draining a leader's accumulated supply of favors very quickly. If the issue is one that party leaders value personally, then we might expect them to spend their owed favors freely and even to accumulate debt; otherwise, leaders have few incentives to spend their earned returns on collective enterprises.

The exercise of discretion runs counter to the tenets of party voting. In fact, discretion expands at the expense of party voting and loyalty. Party loyalty imposes an orthodoxy on party members that discretion-maximizing politicians try to avoid if not ignore. Simply put, the expansion of discretion and the independence it promotes weaken team spirit, thereby reducing party voting.

Team Spirit and Party Voting in the House of Representatives

The above hypotheses can be represented with the following relationship:

$$V = f(L, D, E),$$

where

V = percentage of party votes (percentage of time that at least 50 percent of the Democrats voted against at least 50 percent of the Republicans),[4]

L = size of legislature (number of legislators),

D = expansion of discretion (mean number of committee assignments relative to the number of committees), and

---

4. Data about the Fiftieth to Ninetieth Congress are drawn from Brady, Cooper, and Hurley 1979; data about the Ninety-first to One hundredth Congress are from *Congressional Quarterly Almanac* 1971–89, vols. 26–44.

TABLE 3. Factors Diminishing Team Spirit and Party Voting in the House of Representatives (Standardized Regression Coefficients)

Variables	Eq. 1	Eq. 2
Expansion of discretion	−.36***	−.23*
	(−3.02)[a]	(−1.78)
Number of years since last realignment[b]	−.44***	−.44***
	(−3.61)	(−3.82)
Number of legislators		−.26**
		(−2.19)
Statistics:		
Multiple R^2	.69	.72
R^2	.47	.52
Adjusted R^2	.45	.49
N	51[c]	51[c]
Durbin-Watson statistic	1.64[d]	1.72[d]

[a] T-values are shown in parentheses.

[b] A natural logarithmic transformation has been applied to this variable.

[c] This represents the total number of cases with complete information; the data base comprises fifty-four cases.

[d] Not significant at .05 level.

*Significant at .08 level.   **Significant at .05 level.   ***Significant at .01 level.

E = length of electoral realignment (years since last realignment—1860, 1896, and 1932).

The estimates for these relationships are shown in table 3 and support the above hypotheses. Party voting declines in response to reductions in team spirit brought about by increases in discretion and the passing of a realignment (eq. 1); these variables explain 47 percent of the variation in party voting over time in the House of Representatives. In equation 2, I introduce the size of the legislature into the model. This equation indicates that as the size of a legislature increases, party loyalty also declines. While the addition of this latter variable reduces the effects of discretion and its level of statistical significance, there is sufficient evidence to conclude that the expansion of discretion is a critical factor in reducing party loyalty.

These relationships suggest that party leaders confront serious obstacles in clearing the market and making the legislature productive that stem from the exercise of discretion in a team-production context. Whether or not the exercise of discretion is due to the size of the House and the imperceptibility of members' efforts, disagreements over party policy (growing party factionalism), or the desire of members to maximize their own individual influence, the result is the same: declines in team spirit and low levels of party loyalty. Clearly, making the legislature productive is a difficult task for party leaders since there are many deterrents to party support and team spirit cannot be relied upon to overcome these obstacles. Yet party leaders must keep the legislature productive to earn the returns they value so much.

How Party Leaders Increase Legislative Productivity

If party leaders benefit from clearing the market for legislation and producing laws, they have an incentive to make the legislature as productive as possible, but at the most tolerable personal cost to themselves. One basic cost facing party leaders is that associated with negotiating agreements. The more agreements that must be negotiated, the higher the cost. Committees provide one mechanism for coping with this problem: party leaders reduce some of their costs of doing business by confining their negotiations to committee leaders. Even if party leaders limit their major transactions to committee leaders, one problem remains: how many committees will keep the transaction costs to a tolerable level?

While party leaders might prefer to reduce their transaction costs to the minimum by insisting upon a small number of large-sized committees, they refrain from doing so because large committees intensify the problems associated with team production, such as shirking. These problems set an effective limit on the number of committees in a legislature: leaders cannot reduce their transaction costs below a certain level for fear of encouraging widespread shirking and thereby reducing the productivity of the legislature. Once the decision on the number of committees is made, it becomes a fixed input in the production of legislation because of the difficulty of altering this decision in the short run; such decisions are incorporated into durable rules (e.g., legislative rules) that can only be changed with a high degree of difficulty. This restricts the output of the legislature to a specific isoquant (i.e., level of production).[5] Only by increasing the size of committees can party leaders increase the productivity of the legislature.

An obvious solution to the problem requires party leaders to increase the size of committees, but in a body with a fixed membership, this necessitates increasing the demand for committee assignments. That is, if members accept more committee assignments, the legislature can move to a higher level of law production. In figure 8 a hypothetical legislature is shown, producing at point *P,* with twenty committees and fifteen legislators per committee. With a doubling in the number of members per committee, and retaining the same

---

5. For scholars lacking a familiarity with microeconomics, isoquants represent the locus of points showing all possible combinations of inputs (i.e., committees and committee members) capable of producing a given level of output. An isoquant that lies above another designates a higher level of output (laws).

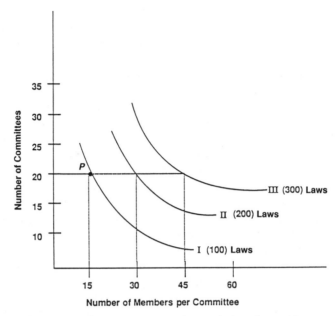

Fig. 8. The relationship between number and size of committees and legislative productivity

number of committees, the legislature is able to produce at a higher level isoquant (II). Clearly, party leaders must increase the demand for assignments to move the legislature to a higher level of productivity.

Party leaders cannot force members to take on the increased responsibilities attached to additional committee assignments without offering some incentive; to do otherwise encourages free riding and shirking or, at the very least, escalates the costs of policing for party leaders. Legislators cannot be motivated to demand more assignments unless they can be assured that their investment (time and effort) in another assignment will be both productive and secure. Rules strengthening the committee system and protecting the discretion of committee members provide the type of assurances that legislators require. For example, the seniority norm (committee members cannot be removed from their committees) assures members continuous access to their committees for as long as they want, assuming no interparty changes in the composition of the legislature:

in the contemporary House a *property-right* is observed according to which a member, once assigned to a committee, has a claim to his committee slot in succeeding Congresses. Within the committees moreover, he has a claim to his position in the seniority queue so that, if he has accrued the most committee seniority, and his party is in the majority, he can expect to be named committee chairman. (Shepsle 1978, 29–30)

Thus, by offering to protect the investments made in committees, party leaders are able to increase productivity (fig. 8). The key is the increased demand for assignments, which, in turn, is dependent upon the degree to which committee investments are secure.

The establishment of a property-rights system, granting committees near-monopoly control over a small set of policies and offering protection to committee membership, seems certain to increase the productivity of the legislature. Some of the gain is the natural result of the specialization among committees created by the assignment of property rights; however, such specialization will not occur until legislators can be convinced that the investment in gaining expertise (time and effort) will be safe from the discretionary actions of party leaders.

Discretion and Lawmaking in the House of Representatives: An Empirical Analysis

In this section I examine propositions drawn from my theory describing relationships among barriers to entry, discretion, rules, and legislative productivity with respect to the House of Representatives. The data span the years 1881 to 1988.

Legislative Productivity

The productivity of Congress (number of pages of laws per day of legislative session)[6] should respond positively to the growth in discretion and electoral safety and negatively to the size of the legislature and the number of uncompensated violations of seniority. The negative relationship between legislature size and legislative productivity reflects the premise that members are likely to shirk their legislative responsibilities when their individual efforts are obscured due to the size of the legislature. As in many collective enterprises, large groups are normally unable to provide collective benefits unless they supply selective benefits and tied sales (of collective and selective benefits) (Olson 1971). The expansion of committee assignments (discretion) overcomes this problem in team production.

William Shugart and Robert Tollison (1986) contend that large-sized leg-

---

6. These data are drawn from counts of the number of pages of laws in the *United States Statutes at Large* 1881–1988, vols. 22–100.

islatures should produce more, rather than fewer, laws because there are fewer voters per legislator, thereby making the task of monitoring the legislator's behavior easier for constituents. This reduces the incentive to shirk. I argue, in contrast, that because most legislative shirking occurs in Washington—away from the watchful eyes of constituents—the dissemination of information is critical to successful monitoring. Since constituents cannot afford the prohibitive costs of monitoring the behavior of legislators while in Washington, they must rely upon other sources to collect this information, such as newspapers. The larger the size of the legislature, the more difficult will be the task of following legislators for most information gatherers; hence, more, not less, shirking should occur in large legislatures.

The positive relationship between electoral safety and productivity is based on the premise that the existence of barriers to entry reduces electoral competition and thereby diminishes the time that members need to devote to electioneering. If the opportunity cost for members reflects the time taken away from legislative interests and pursuits, then electoral safety should free members to devote more time to their lawmaking activities and less time to electioneering. Therefore, electoral safety should increase the resources that members willingly devote to legislative activities, increasing the overall productivity of Congress.

I also include a measure of uncompensated violations of seniority in the selection of House committee leaders. Seniority not only protects members' rights to a committee assignment but it also serves as something of a promissory note that entitles the most-senior committee member to chair the committee. In this way, seniority enhances the value of committee membership. Therefore, members should devote even more time to their committee work when they feel that their commitment will pay off handsomely in the future by the automatic accession to a committee chair. Such devotion may increase the productivity of Congress even beyond what we might expect from the sheer growth in discretion.

Uncompensated violations of seniority in the selection of House committee leaders represent instances where party leaders intervened in the careers of members. This sort of intervention barely survived after the changes in the 1911 rules, vesting the Speaker's jurisdiction over committee assignments in party committees. In fact, violations virtually disappeared between the Seventy-third (1933–34) and One hundredth (1987–88) Congresses, interrupted only by the unusual removal of three committee leaders in the Ninety-fourth Congress (1975–76), and Les Aspin's ascension to chair of the Armed Services Committee ahead of a few more senior Democrats in 1985 (fig. 9).

We specify these relationships as

$$O = f(D, M, L, S),$$

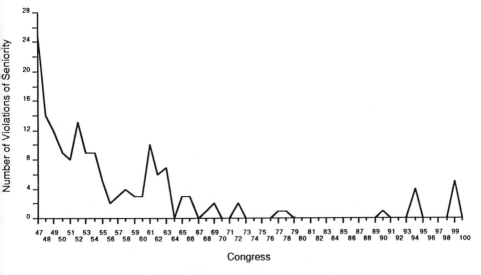

Fig. 9. The number of uncompensated violations of seniority in selecting committee leaders, 1881–1988

where

O = legislative productivity (pages of laws per day in session),

D = expansion of discretion (mean number of committee assignments relative to the number of committees),

M = electoral insecurity (percentage of House incumbents receiving between 45 and 55 percent of the vote),

L = size of legislature (number of legislators), and

S = seniority violations (number of uncompensated violations of seniority in the House).

The trend over time in the number of pages of laws per day in session (days in session minus days in recess) is illustrated in figure 10. The level of legislative output remained under three pages per day from 1881 to 1896 (from the Forty-seventh to the Fifty-fourth Congresses); the Fifty-sixth Congress (1899–1900) set a high point—almost six pages per day—that lasted for the next quarter of a century. From the Forty-seventh to the Fifty-fourth Congress, none of the eight congresses exceeded three pages of laws per day, but from the Fifty-fifth (1897–98) to the Ninety-eighth (1983–84) Congress, only five congresses (the Sixty-second, Sixty-third, Sixty-fifth, Sixty-seventh, and Seventy-seventh Congresses) fell below the three-page level. Another

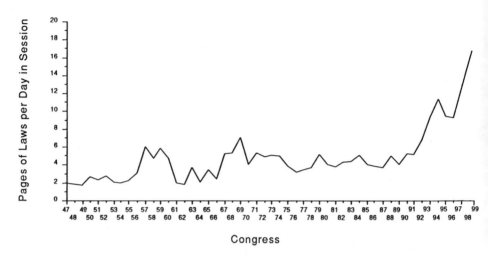

Fig. 10. Legislative productivity

high level of legislative productivity occurred in the Seventieth Congress (1927–28) when over seven pages per day were recorded; this level of productivity was exceeded only recently (from the Ninety-fourth to the One hundredth Congress). Between the Ninety-fourth (1975–76) and One hundredth (1987–88) Congresses, more than nine pages of laws per day were produced by each Congress—the most productive Congresses. Since the Eightieth Congress (1947–48), only the Eighty-second (1951–52) and Eighty-eighth (1963–64) Congresses produced less than four pages of laws per day. Clearly, Congress has become more productive over time despite the increased amount of constituency contact, with recent levels of productivity about five times higher than a century earlier.

It is clear from table 4 that the expansion of discretion is an extremely important influence on the legislative output of Congress. I should also point out that the relationship between the expansion of discretion and legislative productivity is quite robust and the significance of the estimate of the effect is not biased by autocorrelation. As expected, electoral safety increases the resources that legislators devote to lawmaking, thereby increasing the productivity of the House. The size of the legislature and seniority violations also reduce legislative productivity, but neither is statistically significant (eq. 1). Since the Durbin-Watson value is inconclusive in equation 1, I have applied a first-order autoregressive correction to equation 2. The results of equation 2 suggest that the most reliable factor in enhancing the productivity of Congress

TABLE 4.   The Effects of Discretion, Electoral Safety, Seniority Violations, and the Size of The Legislature on Legislative Productivity, 1881–1988

Variables	Eq. 1		Eq. 2	
	T-value	Significance	T-value	Significance
Percentage of marginal districts	−3.37	.002	−1.47	.151
Number of legislators	−1.43	.160	−1.32	.194
Expansion of discretion	2.55	.015	3.04	.005
Seniority violations	−1.47	.151	−0.49	.631
Statistics:				
R^2		.62		.67
Adjusted R^2		.57		.63
N		41[a]		41[a]
Durbin-Watson statistic		1.260		2.30[b]

Note: A natural logarithmic transformation has been applied to legislative productivity.

[a]This represents the total number of cases with complete information; the data base comprises fifty-four cases.

[b]Not significant at .05 level. A first-order autoregressive correction (Cochrane-Orcutt technique) has been applied to this time series to correct for possible autocorrelation.

is the expansion of discretion (i.e., the only variable significant beyond the .01 level).

Conclusion

It is interesting to note that the expansion of discretion is one factor subject to the influence of party leaders: by guaranteeing members that their investments in committees were safe from the actions of party leaders, leaders fostered the expansion of committee assignments and thereby increased the productivity of the House. Party leaders clearly have less effect on the other influences related to legislative productivity. Neither the size of the legislature nor the level of electoral safety among party members is likely to be affected by the actions of party leaders. Moreover, seniority violations, which party leaders might manipulate to increase productivity, cannot be relied upon to increase the productivity of Congress—i.e., they have a low level of statistical significance (table 4). In sum, the best way for party leaders to keep the legislature productive, and gain returns for doing so, is to institute safeguards that protect the investments of members in their congressional committees. The resulting expansion in discretion, while diminishing party loyalty and team spirit, is capable of moving the legislature to a higher level of productivity. If the recent upsurge in legislative productivity represents a lasting shift rather than a periodic disturbance, we might conclude that party leaders are well aware of the benefits derived from the expansion of discretion by party members. Clearly, higher levels of party loyalty would reduce the costs to leaders and therefore increase their returns, but these gains must be weighed against the losses in productivity that might result from restricting the discretion of party members.

CHAPTER 4

Economic Incentives to Congressional Service

There are a number of collective benefits that legislative scholars typically associate with long congressional tenure, such as policy expertise, and one of the benefits of discretion-maximization is that it has enhanced the attractiveness of congressional service. Members want to stay in Congress because their investments in the committee system accrue value, perhaps yielding a choice committee chair in due time. There are other factors that make long congressional careers attractive, such as the salary associated with the job, the nonpecuniary returns available, and the rents collected from interest groups and other favor buyers. But before discussing the economic incentives to congressional service, it is important to briefly summarize some of the major explanations for the increased longevity of members that do not rely upon economic motivations or incentives.

Some Historical Explanations
for Congressional Careerism

Why congressional careers have lengthened (Polsby 1985) has sparked considerable speculation (see, for instance, Brookshire and Duncan 1983), but as Nobel economist George Stigler notes, "there does not appear to be a satisfactory theory of legislative tenure. The more than doubling of the average term of Congressmen in the last hundred years . . . has not been explained" (1976, 31). Many explanations account for increasing congressional tenure in terms of historical electoral conditions: the lower the overall level of electoral safety, the more turnover in membership, and therefore the shorter congressional careers become.

Two general trends in turnover in the House of Representatives are apparent: turnover increased until the 1850s and has declined since that time (Fiorina, Rohde, and Wissel 1975). This gross change in the membership of the House masks some interesting variations in the turnover rate. There was, for example, considerable fluctuation in the turnover rate in the early Congresses, with a distinct upward trend in turnover visible until the Seventeenth or Eighteenth Congress. House turnover rates stabilized around the middle of the 1850s before beginning a rather erratic decline. The turnover rate reached another high point in the Fifty-fourth Congress (1895–96) but again declined. Turnover rose a little during the Woodrow Wilson presidency, then dropped to another low point in the Seventieth Congress (after the election of 1926), before increasing with the approach of the Great Depression and the 1932 landslide election of Franklin D. Roosevelt. During the 1970s, turnover in the House appears to increase slightly, though the level of turnover still remained below the levels reached before 1950.

These patterns in the turnover rate tend to coincide with historical changes in the electoral domination of one of the major parties. On the basis of differences in the degree and nature of party competition, political historians define five periods in the development of the present-day party system in the United States. The first party system encompasses the years between 1788 and 1824 and features the dominance of the Republican party after the Federalist party began to disappear as an effective opposition party (after 1808); during this period of dominance, Republicans won from 61 to 85 percent of the House seats. The second party system, 1824–54, crumbled with the rise of the Republican party in the elections of 1854 and 1856.

In the Civil War system, 1860–92, Republicans were in control until 1874, after which control of the presidency and Congress alternated between the parties. The Civil War weakened the Democratic party outside of the South, as Democratic candidates suffered from the party's association with the Southern cause. This weakness in the Democratic party helped Republicans maintain control of the presidency until 1885, of the Senate until 1897, and of the House until 1875. The polarization of the country along sectional lines in the 1890s marks the end of the Civil War party system.

During the fourth party era, 1896–1932, Republicans maintained domination until 1912, when Theodore Roosevelt's Bull Moose Progressive movement split Republican loyalties and provided presidential victories for Woodrow Wilson and the Democratic party. Republican domination returned, however, in 1920 and lasted until FDR's election in 1932, the start of the fifth party system. There is no consensus among political historians as to the end of the fifth party system and the start of the sixth, but some suggest that a major realignment in the parties brought to a close the fifth party system in 1968. Regardless of whether we are in the fifth or sixth party system, it seems clear that the instability and decay of party systems can promote high levels of turnover in Congress, thereby reducing the length of many congressional careers.

Structural changes in the electoral system also affect turnover. H. D. Price argues, for example, that the election of 1896 was particularly critical in altering levels of congressional turnover:

> This decade was marked by the emergence of the really solid Democratic South, by the rapid spread of ballot reform and registration systems, but

above all by the collapse of the Democrats in the 1896 Bryan campaign. Democratic gains in the silver states and some farming states proved temporary, but massive Democratic losses in the Northeast and Mid-west were to last until Al Smith and the Great Depression. As a result, re-election became more probable and more incumbents came to seek re-election. Successive new all-time records for amount of prior service in the House were set in 1900, then a higher record in 1904, then a yet higher record in 1906, and that one was broken in 1908. Successive new all-time low records for proportion of new members were set in 1898, again in 1900, again in 1904, and yet again in 1908. (1975, 9)

In addition to the competitiveness of party systems and the existence of critical elections, historical patterns of membership turnover can be linked to the attractiveness of Congress as a decision-making body and the decline of local norms that once required incumbents to retire after short periods of service.

It is customary to think of the Senate as one of the nation's most powerful political institutions, and certainly more powerful than the House, because of its constitutional role in foreign affairs and executive branch appointments. However, Price reminds us that in its initial decades the Senate was little more than an "honorific nothing" (1975, 6). After the Civil War and Reconstruction, the attractiveness of the Senate increased as the institution reached a pinnacle of influence:

The executive branch was in a long eclipse, and senators extended their sway into effective control of state party machines (or vice versa). The national government was by then of vital importance in regard to tariff policy, monetary policy, and—for the South—race policy. Senators controlled the allocation of federal patronage, and increasingly lorded it over the House. Thus by the 49th Congress (1885) resignations were only one-third the number of 1845, though the Senate was twenty members larger. The ratio of members seeking re-election to those not doing so is no longer half and half, but stands at 55 to 13. By this time most states were predominantly either Democratic or Republican, so that electoral hazards were reduced. By this time also, Senate committee chairmanships were being quite rigorously handled in terms of continuous committee service. The Senate was a good place for a politician to be. (1975, 8–9)

The attractiveness of the House of Representatives also increased for some of the same reasons, especially the enhanced role of the House in the formation of public policy. One example of the enhanced role of the House in the making of major policy decisions was the creation of tariff barriers to protect specific domestic industries. Not only did the tariff question give each member a constituency-stake in the issue and influence over national policies but the tariff produced substantial budget surpluses for members to spend (Kernell 1977, 674). Thus, the job of the representative became more important and more prestigious. Increased congressional tenure is indicative of the desire of incumbents to continue to serve in Congress, and the improved status of the House and the Senate were indeed handsome incentives to return to Washington.

Another historical factor responsible for some of the decline in congressional turnover was the norm of rotation: the rotation of the nomination for a congressional seat among party faithfuls for specific periods of time. These rotation practices declined during the last half of the nineteenth century and disappeared by the twentieth, but in the interim they increased congressional turnover (Kernell 1977). Two forces that hastened the demise of the rotation norm were the challenges on the part of enterprising incumbents and the substitution of the direct primary, on a national scale, for the party caucus in the selection of nominees for office. By loading the district conventions with supportive delegates or by exploiting access to patronage appointments, incumbents occasionally succeeded in overturning the traditional two-term limit on their careers. Direct primaries virtually liberated incumbents from dependence upon unpredictable caucuses for their nominations, allowing them to exploit their proven campaign skills and the resources of their offices to maximum electoral and political advantage.

An Economic Approach to Congressional Careerism

The preceding paragraphs describe several historical explanations for the lengthening of terms of office, but this analysis pursues a different line of inquiry: the economic incentives to congressional service and the rational behavior of discretion-maximizing legislators. These, I believe, motivated both past and present members to stay in Congress and to run for reelection again and again.

Rent Extractions

Monetary incentives for congressional careers come in a variety of forms. Simply put, money talks! Not all of a legislator's pay is above the table; outside-the-legislature pay comes in a variety of legal, quasi-legal, and illegal forms. One source of pay can be termed a *rent*. A rent is defined as a payment to a factor of production (e.g. a legislator) in excess of that factor's opportunity cost. In the economic approach to interest-group theory (see, for example, McCormick and Tollison 1981), legislators act as passive brokers creating rents and returns that interest groups compete to capture. Legislators can also force payments on the side from these groups by threatening them with taxes and/or regulations designed to expropriate their specific capital.

One example of how legislators gain from threatening regulation, and later removing that threat in exchange for a fee, is the used-car rule of the Federal Trade Commission (FTC). At the insistence of Congress, the FTC initiated efforts to regulate used-car dealers' warranties; the result was a rule imposing costly warranty and auto-defect disclosure requirements. This rule created the opportunity for legislators to extract concessions from dealers to void the burdensome measures, since Congress had in the interim legislated for itself a veto over FTC actions. Once the rule was promulgated, used-car dealers and their trade associations descended on Congress, seeking relief from the proposed rule. Congress then vetoed the very rule it had ordered, earning legislators handsome rents (McChesney 1987, 114). "In the House, 186 of the 216 representatives who cosponsored the resolution to overturn the regulation had received [campaign] contributions from the auto dealers in the previous three years. Sixteen members became cosponsors within ten days of receiving their contributions" (Berry 1984, 172). The inactivity of legislators in passing tax legislation is another prime example of how legislators can elicit private payments for not imposing costs on affected interests. "Recently, the excise tax on beer has generated substantial revenue for legislators in return for their inactivity" (McChesney 1987, 115–16).

Legislators, therefore, both create and extract rents. Cynically put, legislators troll the economy looking for ways to propose regulations and taxation, not so much to correct social ills but to fill their own pockets or their campaign coffers. Thus, the ability to extract rents from groups and individuals should motivate legislators to seek long congressional careers.

In an electorally competitive situation, we might expect these rents to quickly dissipate, as potential officeholders attempt to outbid each other for the support of electorally important interest groups by promising to reduce "their take." In the absence of durable rules and institutional constraints (see chapter 6), electorally safe members have no reason to reduce their rent extractions for helping groups in the district because entry barriers reduce competitive bidding; hence, rents are unlikely to dissipate under the noncompetitive electoral conditions that presently characterize the vast number of congressional districts.[1] In short, where barriers to entry exist, rent extractions should be unusually profitable and therefore provide incentives for establishing long congressional careers.

---

1. About three-quarters of the incumbents running for reelection won with at least 60 percent of the vote since the late 1960s (Ornstein, Mann, and Malbin 1990).

Salary

It is a basic economic principle that monetary remuneration is an important incentive. Therefore, congressional salaries are a likely selling point in encouraging members to establish long congressional tenure. Article 1, Section G, of the Constitution provides that "Senators and Representatives shall receive a compensation for their services, to be ascertained by law, and paid out of the Treasury of the United States." In trying to minimize the adverse political fallout inevitable from periodically raising their own salaries, legislators have instituted the practice of incorporating their pay raises in general pay legislation that grants pay raises for most government workers, including at times the judiciary and the president! Public opposition to congressional pay increases has been unusually strong, leading to wholesale electoral defeats of many legislators who supported increases. On two occasions, salary increases were even repealed by succeeding Congresses. Despite such antipathy toward congressional pay hikes, congressional salaries have risen steadily, particularly in recent years when barriers to entry rose even higher due to a change in product advertising on the part of House and Senate incumbents.

The growth of congressional salaries did, indeed, emerge from humble beginnings. One of the first, and most controversial, measures enacted by the Congress in 1789 was a bill fixing the compensation of members at $6 a day. This bill also provided the first of many congressional perquisites: a travel allowance of $6 per each twenty miles. In 1816, Congress voted itself a pay increase and a shift from per diem compensation to an annual salary: $1,500 a year, with the raise retroactive to the beginning of the session (December 4, 1815). Despite the easy passage, the public outcry was intense and resulted in a number of voluntary and involuntary departures from Congress. In 1817, Congress repealed the $1,500 salary, effective at the end of the Fourteenth Congress (March 3, 1817); in 1818, per diem compensation was restored at the rate of $8 per day, retroactive to March 3, 1817.

Nearly four decades after Congress returned to a per diem compensation scheme, Congress again converted to annual salaries. In 1856, a $3,000 annual salary (retroactive to December 3, 1855—the start of the Thirty-fourth Congress) replaced per diem compensation; another retroactive pay increase followed in 1866, effective as of December 4, 1865 (when the Thirty-ninth Congress convened), that pushed congressional salaries to $5,000. Still another retroactive pay raise was enacted in the closing days of the Forty-second Congress in 1873, increasing salaries to $7,500, with the raise in effect since the beginning of the Forty-second Congress—a $5,000 windfall. This last raise was repealed in 1874 when congressional pay was reduced to $5,000. Salaries rose again in 1907 ($7,500) and 1925 ($10,000), but the Great Depression led to subsequent paycuts; hence, in 1932, salaries were reduced to $9,000 and dropped even further ($8,500) as a result of the Economy Act of March 20, 1933. These cutbacks were gradually rescinded so that by the end of 1935, congressional salaries returned to their 1925 level of $10,000.

The Legislative Reorganization Act of 1946 contained, among its many reform-oriented provisions, an increase in congressional salaries ($12,500) and a provision retaining an existing $2,500 nontaxable expense allowance for all members; the tax-free expense allowance was eliminated in 1951. In 1955, congressional (as well as judicial) salaries were again raised. This time, congressional salaries increased to $22,500. This salary level remained in effect until 1964, when salaries were raised to $30,000.

In 1967 Congress established the nine-member Commission on Executive, Legislative, and Judicial Salaries to recommend salary changes. The commission was created to relieve incumbents of the politically risky task of having to raise their own salaries. The commission was to submit recommendations to the president, who was to propose the exact rates of pay in the annual budget; these rates could be higher or lower than those proposed by the commission. The recommendations were to take effect within thirty days unless Congress either disapproved of part or all of the recommendations or enacted a separate pay measure. This procedure led to an increase in salary to $42,500 in 1969.

Despite this seemingly blame-escaping mechanism, with its blue-ribbon commission, presidential recommendation, and legislative veto features, congressional support for establishing the commission was exceedingly weak. On the House floor the proposal to establish the commission encountered stiff opposition from those fearing that it gave undue power to the president. A similar argument caused the Senate Post Office and Civil Service Committee to drop the idea of a quadrennial commission from the Federal Salary Act of 1967 (Public Law 90-206), and the Senate took no action to reinstate the proposal on the Senate floor (Davidson 1980, 76–78). Still, the House provision was restored in the House-Senate conference when Senate conferees backed down from their opposition to the quadrennial commission.

Since Congress first considered the salary recommendations of the commission, compensation bills have been greeted by a loud chorus of objections by individual legislators. Clearly, such protests may serve no other purpose than to demonstrate legislators' commitment to governmental economy and self-denial. In any event, legislative support for pay raises seems to come from those legislators who are fortunate enough to represent districts with high barriers to entry: electorally safe and senior members of Congress (Davidson 1980, 86). (See Hibbing 1988 and Wilkerson 1990 for analyses of the effect in the Senate of proximity to reelection and voting on tax benefits.)

Although congressional salaries were not increased for almost seven years, a flurry of increases followed. In 1975 Congress approved a cost-of-living increase for itself. The adjustment was tied to a government-wide pay raise. As part of this salary package, Congress opted to make itself (and other top government officials) eligible for the annual October cost-of-living pay raise without having to vote the raise; it would be provided automatically unless incumbents declined to take it. As a result, congressional salaries grew another 5 percent, bringing salaries to $44,600 annually, but the automatic increase in 1976 was passed up. In 1977, Congress seemed prepared to make up for lost time and ground by raising their salaries another $12,500, increasing the congressional salary to $57,500—a pay hike of 29 percent. Members of Congress, however, declined the 1977 cost-of-living increase, a decision repeated again in 1978.

With the beginning of 1979, congressional salaries were $57,500, but an automatic 7 percent increase under cost-of-living procedures would go into effect in October; moreover, legislators also planned to recoup the 5.5 percent increase for 1978 that had been suspended, not repealed. Thus, if Congress took no action, legislators would receive both pay hikes, for a total increase of 12.9 percent. This increase was rolled back to 5.5 percent, bringing congressional salaries up to $60,662.50 beginning in 1980.

Shying away from a vote on an outright pay increase for 1981, Congress devised indirect methods for achieving future pay increases. It approved a procedure whereby members could receive the annual government-wide cost-of-living pay increase without having to vote on the raise; this procedure was approved in October 1981, to take effect October 1, 1982, as a rider attached to an emergency funding bill. Eliminating congressional votes on salary increases was a good way for members to ensure their sanctity since Congress had blocked increases that required a vote in 1977, 1978, 1980, and 1981. In the same legislation containing the automatic cost-of-living adjustment procedure, Congress approved a change in tax laws that enabled incumbents to deduct from their income taxes the expenses they incurred while residing in Washington. Under a 1952 law, the maximum deduction was set at $3,000; the new legislation increased deductions for members by at least $16,000. In response to public pressure, Congress repealed the deduction in 1982, restoring the $3,000 annual limit in force since 1981. Annual increases boosted salaries during the next several years: $72,600 (1984); $75,100 (1985); $77,400 (1986), and $89,500 (1987).

This brief history of the increases in congressional salaries suggests that one economic incentive to the lengthening of congressional careers might be the salary incumbents receive.[2] Of course, there are other sources of income,

---

2. While legislators might be expected to keep their salaries low to deter competition (see, for example, McCormick and Tollison 1981, 79–100), the high levels of electoral security experienced by incumbents probably countered the impulse to create another barrier to entry. Many barriers already existed, and in any event, the marginal gain in electoral security resulting

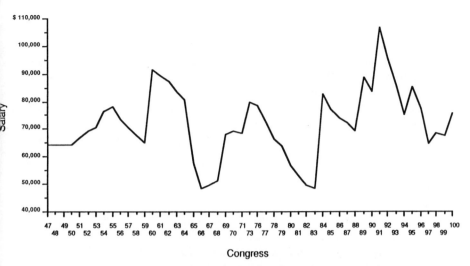

Fig. 11. Comparing the salaries of U.S. Representatives, 1881–1988. No calculations are made for the following Congresses: 72, 74, and 75. Salaries are adjusted by the GNP deflator (1982 = 100).

not the least of which are the fees and royalties (honoraria) that incumbents receive for making public appearances and speeches (see Parker 1992). Besides fees, members often receive expense-paid trips to the sites where their speeches are given, as well as lodging and meals. Until 1975, some members reported earning more income through honoraria than from their congressional salaries! In sum, there are definite financial rewards to congressional service. I should point out, however, that in terms of 1982 dollars, and adjusting for changes in the Gross National Product, congressional salaries do not reveal much of a monotonic change (fig. 11). The fluctuations appear more like ebbs and flows reflecting adjustments in salaries resulting from erosion due to inflation.

Size of the Legislature

The size of the legislature can also provide incentives for members to establish long congressional careers by promoting or constraining shirking. Large legislatures facilitate shirking in at least two closely related ways. First,

---

from foregoing salary increases could not overcome the loss in salary. Therefore, legislators raised their salaries, hoping that few constituents would be outraged by the action but feeling secure that their existing level of electoral safety could withstand a mild revolt. The gain in salary, in short, was perceived as worth the electoral risk, especially in light of growing electoral safety.

because a member's effort is imperceptible in a large legislature, a rational member can shirk without worrying about the lack of effort becoming noticed. Second, monitoring and metering the behavior of members impose high costs on congressional leaders in large legislatures. The greater the number of members in a legislature, the more difficult the tasks of monitoring (the higher the cost), and as a result, the greater the incentives for shirking by legislators. Simply put, legislators in large legislatures can purchase more leisure than those in small legislatures. The increased opportunities to shirk in large legislatures should provide an incentive to stay in office; such shirking can translate into congressional junkets and hunts for honoraria and rents.

Expansion of Discretion

One of the positive benefits of the expansion in discretion is that it has made legislative life more attractive. The capacity to give free expression to values and beliefs and to pursue personal objectives make discretion a valued commodity—and a factor in why members are staying in office longer. Certainly, the expansion of discretion introduces some inefficiency into the decision-making process by reducing team loyalty and the influence of such centralizing forces as presidents and party leaders; it does, however, have other assets that keep legislatures operating smoothly.

Discretionary behavior is not entirely wasteful because it reduces efficiency in the legislative process. The ability to exercise discretion enhances the stability of Congress by strengthening morale and fueling ambition; such stability is beneficial to all types of organizations and institutions. Downs makes a similar point about waste in bureaucracies:

> From the viewpoint of people outside the bureau, any of its activities not directed at carrying out its social functions comprise wasted motion. By this standard, a significant portion of every bureau's activities are wasteful. . . . Some types of wasted motion have important positive functions. For example, certain actions by every official serve purely personal goals. From the viewpoint of people outside the bureau, these actions seem to be 100 percent waste. However they provide the official with important personal satisfactions which contribute to his morale. Such satisfactions as socialization and small talk, improving personal comfort, and resisting orders that disrupt pleasant habits form a significant part of every official's incentives for staying in the bureau and performing his official tasks effectively. . . . In order to accomplish its formal goals, every organization must undertake many activities that have no direct connection with those goals, but that are aimed at maintaining the coalition of individuals necessary to achieve them. (1967, 136–7)

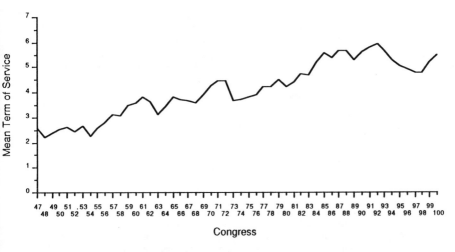

Fig. 12. Mean term of congressional service in the House of Representatives, 1881–1988

Legislatures, like Downs's bureaus, benefit from the institutional slack that creates opportunities for members to exercise discretion.

Why Careerism Has Grown in the House of Representatives

The growth over time in the mean term of congressional service within the House of Representatives is depicted in figure 12. A steady growth in terms of service is revealed in the figure: House members were serving less than three terms prior to the Fifty-seventh Congress (1901–2), but tenure steadily rose after that point, reaching the highest level during the entire series in the Ninety-second Congress (1971–72)—nearly six terms (twelve years). There was a slight decline in careerism between the Ninety-sixth (1979–80) and Ninety-eighth (1983–84) Congresses to pre-1955 levels, but the series rebounded in the Ninety-ninth (1985–86) and One hundredth (1987–88) Congresses.

Any economic explanation for careerism must take into account four factors: salary, rent extractions, the size of the legislature, and the expansion of discretion. Increases in salary and the capacity for rent extractions provide strong monetary incentives to stay in Congress and establish lengthy careers. The size of the legislature influences levels of shirking; hence, as the size of the House of Representatives increased, so did the opportunities for shirking. And the greater the opportunities for shirking, the more attractive a congres-

TABLE 5.   Explaining Terms of Service in the House of Representatives

Variables	T-value	Significance
Pages of private bills[a]	1.77	.084
Congressional salary	1.25	.218
Number of legislators	8.25	.000
Expansion of discretion	7.19	.000
Statistics:		
R^2	.93	
Adjusted R^2	.93	
N	49[b]	
Durbin-Watson statistic	1.73[c]	

Note: A first-order autoregressive correction (Cochrane-Orcutt technique) has been applied to the time series to correct for serial correlation.

[a] A natural logarithmic transformation has been applied to this variable.

[b] This represents the total number of cases with complete information; the data base comprises fifty-four cases.

[c] Not significant at .05 level.

sional career should look. Thus, size of the legislature should be positively related to terms of congressional service. Finally, the expansion of discretion (fig. 6) should enhance the attractiveness of Congress and motivate incumbents to establish long congressional careers.

These relationships can be expressed as

$$T = f(X, L, R, D),$$

where

   T = mean terms of congressional service,
   X = congressional salary (adjusted by GNP deflator, 1982 = 100),
   L = size of legislature (number of legislators),
   R = opportunity to collect rents (pages of private bills), and
   D = expansion of discretion (mean number of committee assignments relative to the number of committees).

The above relationships are estimated in table 5.

It appears from table 5 that monetary incentives are less important in promoting lengthy careers than those associated with shirking (which is related to the size of the legislature) and the expansion of discretion. Private bills are legislation submitted by members of Congress on behalf of groups or individual constituents. The specific nature of this legislation (singling out

TABLE 6.   Impact of Government Service on Salaries (salaries adjusted to 1967 constant dollars)

Office	Before Government	At Entry to Government	First Job after Government
Executive appointees	41,318	29,095	46,738
Executives (levels 1–4)	43,624	29,339	48,883
Members of Congress	28,483	26,864	41,421
Judges	42,791	24,085	45,489

Source: U.S. Congress, House 1977a, 433.

and naming individuals for relief) makes such bills prime opportunities to extract a rent or two.[3] The capacity to process such bills increases the attractiveness of Congress but, like congressional salaries, fails to exercise a statistically significant influence on careerism. The equation, nonetheless, does a remarkable job in explaining the growth in terms of service in the House ($R^2 = .93$), and the significance of the estimates do not appear to be biased by autocorrelation (table 5). The expansion of discretion, as I have frequently noted, may mean plunder as well as altruism. If the lengthening of careers is an expression of the satisfaction derived from office holding, then the monetary consequences of expanding discretion seem to be of only negligible importance.[4]

From the data in table 6 it can be inferred why the monetary incentives to congressional service might not lengthen careers in Congress. This table is based on a survey conducted in late 1976 of former federal executives, judges, and members of Congress regarding their salaries before and after government employment. These figures suggest that members of Congress experienced the greatest change between their salaries before and after government employment, and they are the only group to show more than a marginal gain in their before-government salary *after* government service. It is clear from this table that only some of the gains to be obtained from a congressional career can be captured while in office. In short, there is a considerable monetary (economic) incentive to enter legislative service, but a large amount of this

---

3. As an extreme example of the ability to use private legislation to extract rents from constituents, former representative Henry Helstroski (D—New Jersey, 1965–76) was indicted for taking bribes in exchange for introducing private bills allowing aliens to immigrate into, or remain in, the United States.

4. I should also point out that the accumulation of committee assignments on the part of House and Senate incumbents appears unrelated to the "extra pay" of legislator—honoraria. That is, the number of committee assignments held by a House or Senate incumbent has no statistically significant relationship to the amount of honoraria income earned (Parker 1992).

gain can only be captured *after* employment. Thus, some of the monetary incentives for legislative service require members to leave office to capture the benefits, thereby reducing, not lengthening, congressional careers.

Conclusion

One of the positive benefits of the expansion of discretion is that it has enhanced the attractiveness of Congress and increased tenure. I recognize that such stability is not without its costs. This conclusion is not intended to bolster arguments over the value of long congressional tenure. I only want to suggest that the expansion of discretion has made Congress a more attractive place to pursue a career. While such discretion does not preclude the pursuit of financial gain, I find little support for the contention that financial considerations play a major role in the lengthening of terms of service.

CHAPTER 5

Constraints on Discretion

Even with barriers to entry in place, members of Congress cannot hope to expand their discretion without diligent personal attention to constituency problems; otherwise, they will be unable to successfully differentiate their products and reduce the attractiveness of substitutes. Service to constituents is an output or product furnished by the member; hence, it behaves like most products—it is influenced by cost and demand. That is, the level of service to the district is a function of constituents' demand for service and the cost of providing such service:

$$C = f(P, W),$$

where

C = service to constituents and the district,
P = cost of the service supplied to the district and its inhabitants, and
W = demand for services.

We might expect the costs of constituency service to serve as an effective constraint on the expansion of discretion. Expanding discretion requires increased vote surpluses; such surpluses are related to the number of constituents reached through the legislator's services or the personal advertising of those services. The amount of discretion consumed should increase as long as the marginal return in votes exceeds the marginal cost of providing the constituency-pleasing service essential for producing vote surpluses.[1]

---

1. In a purely competitive situation, marginal return (*MR*) equals price (*P*), and the demand curve is the marginal return curve. The competitive situation requires producers to maximize profits by producing where $P = MC$ (marginal cost). Although both competitive and monopoly conditions lead producers to follow the same rule, $MR = MC$, the result is fundamentally different. To maximize profits, the monopolist follows the same rule that the competitive firm follows—it sets marginal cost equal to marginal return. The logic is also identical in both cases: if *MR* is greater than *MC*, it pays to produce additional services because they add more to revenues than to costs. If *MR* is less than *MC*, it pays to reduce production because extra output adds more to costs than to revenues. Marginal return is *not* the same as price for the monopolist; the

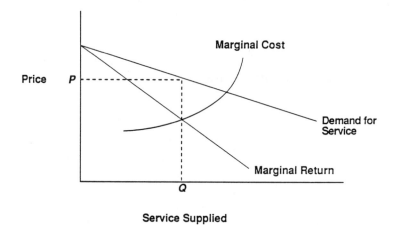

Service Supplied

Fig. 13. Cost constraints on discretion-maximization

How the costs of service might indirectly constrain attempts to expand discretion is shown in figure 13. Members, behaving as monopolists in supplying constituency service, expand their output of services as long as marginal return (MR) exceeds marginal cost (MC). Thus, the output of services will be expanded to point Q, where $MR = MC$ (fig. 13). To provide a quantity of services greater than Q, the monopolist's cost of producing more services will be greater than the marginal gain in votes (i.e., the marginal return [revenue] curve is below the marginal cost curve); hence, the monopolist restricts his or her level of service to Q. This sets a limit on the level of vote surplus that the incumbent can accumulate and, therefore, the expansion of discretion. Without an effective cost constraint, legislators maximize *total* returns rather than *marginal* gain; under this latter condition, legislators have every incentive to expand their services regardless of the returns. In fact, rational legislators should expand their services until virtually no returns are forthcoming!

The Costs of Constituency Service

In the market, cost considerations would normally set severe constraints on the production of constituency service. However, the costs to members of Congress associated with the services supplied constituents are minimal, after the initial start-up costs required in assembling a legislative staff and estab-

---

monopolist produces where $P > MC$. The profit-maximizing price for the monopolist is represented by the horizontal line intersecting the demand curve at the point on that curve directly above the intersection of the marginal cost and return curves (see fig. 13).

lishing office routines. Moreover, members do not have to bear all the costs of such service because Congress has subsidized a large amount of the resources needed to respond to constituents' demands (e.g., staff, travel expenses, and mass mailings). If legislators view their legislative tasks as their highest-valued opportunity (Parker 1989a), they do not incur major opportunity costs in attending to district needs—they rarely have to sacrifice their legislative interests. Staff can shoulder much of the responsibility for district service, which means that legislators can expand their enterprises and perform more services for constituents without having to shoulder all of the additional burden. Perhaps equally important, Congress has structured the legislative schedule so that legislative business doesn't conflict with personal contact with constituents and therefore doesn't increase the opportunity costs associated with constituency attention. Most legislative business takes place between Tuesday and Thursday, so legislators can spend time with their constituents without having to miss important legislative activity; recess periods have multiplied during the past few decades, which also allows members more opportunities to spend time in their districts without neglecting legislative interests (Fig. 5).

We might also envision the overproduction of constituency service as constraining the expansion of discretion. The minimal costs attached to the supply of constituency service (for legislators) and the value of the output in promoting political leeway provide ample incentives for members to constantly expand the volume (and perhaps range) of constituency service. In the marketplace, such overproduction would hurt the producer: the consumer eventually gains less value from each additional unit of the commodity (or service) consumed, and therefore the marginal utility derived declines as the rate of utilization increases.

Extending this logic to the provision of constituency service, we might expect legislators to suffer from the overproduction of this service: the pervasiveness and volume lead voters to attribute less importance to the activity, thereby diminishing its value to the individual voter. Perhaps voters become saturated with messages about the service provided by the incumbent representative to the point that additional messages of this kind fail to gain attention or support. As a consequence, political issues could replace constituency service as a means of differentiating between candidates, thereby reducing the incumbent's ability to maneuver in Washington and to exercise discretion.

While the pervasiveness of constituency service might reduce its value to constituents, there is no empirical evidence that this has occurred or is likely to occur in the future. Constituency attention is the most frequently mentioned basis for liking or disliking a representative, and the vast number of these references are quite positive (Parker and Davidson 1979). Furthermore, other criteria that might gain relevance in voters' decisions, such as issues or ideology, remain infrequently mentioned. Why, then, does the provision of constituency service remain such a highly valued commodity despite its growth and pervasiveness (Fiorina 1977)?

The inclination of legislators to "run for Congress by running against Congress" (Fenno 1978, 168)—attacking the institution—provides an explanation for the centrality of constituency service in voters' evaluations. Fenno (1978) calls attention to the willingness of members to assail legislative practices, the behavior of others in Congress, and the institution itself. This strategy enables individual members to differentiate themselves from others in Congress and to portray themselves as fighters against its institutional shortcomings (Fenno 1978, 167).

The adoption of this strategy is especially appealing because it entails few costs. For instance, attacking Congress is an effective way for members to endear themselves to their own constituents.

> Congress and its members are remote, cold abstractions. Collectively and individually they can be attacked at home without fear of constituency disfavor. To the contrary, because most constituents are critical of Congress to begin with, the congressman stands only to increase constituent identification and trust when he joins—and leads—the chorus. (Fenno 1978, 166–67)

Legislators, then, run for Congress by demonstrating that they are *solely* and *personally* responsible for the services received by voters. As noted earlier, such behavior (a legislator differentiating his or her product) reduces the elasticity of demand for the incumbent's constituency service.

And the message is a convincing one at election time since actions speak louder than words (Downs 1957, 106): incumbents can point to their records of constituency service, but challengers have only promises to elicit voters' support. The choice in this situation is clear: voters would prefer to continue the flow of constituency service to the district than to chance the possibility (which voters see as quite unlikely) that an incumbent's replacement will do as well. By attacking the institution and ridiculing the others in Congress, incumbents also escape the blame for whatever problem is plaguing the vast majority of their constituents. At the same time, it enables legislators to emphasize their services to constituents and to remind them of the legislators' personal responsibility for the delivery of those services. This promotes the impression that the incumbent is the *only one* who can, and will, cater to the needs of the district, thus elevating the performance of that service in the minds of voters and distinguishing the candidates. In low-information contests where it is difficult to differentiate candidates on the basis of their policy stands, like most congressional contests, such considerations can dominate voters' decisions.

In conclusion, incumbents exploit consumers' distrust and uncertainty to keep their constituency service highly valued: they convince voters that there is no *substitute* for their attention. In this way constituency service never loses its attraction for the individual citizen, and legislators need never worry about overproducing. This is not to imply that there are no cost constraints on the expansion of discretion. Indeed, the *personal* attention and contact of legislators are limited by their time and energies, which are distinctly finite. This naturally sets a limit on the size of their vote surpluses. And, of course, there are the opportunity costs associated with personal attention to constituent problems; these costs may, in fact, exercise the most severe constraints on the expansion of discretion by individual legislators. Simply put, legislators must forego opportunities to pursue their own personal interests in Washington when giving personal attention to constituency matters. Such opportunity costs are probably directly related to a legislator's position in the institutional hierarchy; hence, the more institutional power a member holds, the greater the sacrifice he or she has to make in attending to constituent matters. For instance, senators in general are more powerful than representatives because of the smaller size of the Senate as compared to the House of Representatives, and the rules of the Senate that accord greater institutional influence to individual senators (e.g., the right to filibuster). Not surprisingly, senators spend less time personally visiting with voters in their states than do representatives (Parker 1986). In sum, legislators undertake constituent activities essential to expanding their own discretion only as long as those services do not significantly disrupt or interfere with the actual exercise of discretion. Beyond this point, the marginal cost of these services exceeds the marginal return.

Despite the existence of significant opportunity costs, the lack of electoral constraints (due to the existence of barriers to entry) on members of Congress might lead to the conclusion that there are no explicit limits to the discretion-maximizing behavior of legislators. Such fears are unwarranted. Shepsle and Weingast (1981) call attention to the importance of rules and institutional arrangements in constraining legislative choice. Not surprisingly, institutional rules also constrain the expansion of discretion and have prevented discretion-maximizing behavior from leading to the long-term collapse of the legislature. Two institutional constraints are of particular note: (1) congressional ethics and financial disclosure laws and (2) the proliferation of restrictive rules in the House of Representatives. These constraints set effective limits on the exercise of discretion.

Congressional Ethics

There might not seem to be much rationale for members of Congress to institute durable rules relating to their own ethics that limit their discretion, but that has happened, and it seems certain to happen in the future. Indeed,

TABLE 7. House Members' Views of Financial Disclosure Requirements

Category of Response[a]	Percentage
Much too stringent	1
Somewhat too stringent	4
Somewhat too loose	31
Much too loose	32
Neither too loose nor too stringent (volunteered)	32
Not sure	0

Source: U.S. Congress, House 1977a, 904.

Note: One hundred and forty-six members surveyed.

[a]Question: "Would you say that present disclosure requirements are much too stringent, somewhat too stringent, that they are somewhat too loose, or that they are much too loose?"

there seems to be considerable support among House members for even more stringent controls on the personal conduct of members: in a survey of House incumbents conducted in 1977, 60 percent felt that rules should be changed to require a full disclosure of finances, and 66 percent supported restrictions on outside income (U.S. Congress, House 1977b, 905–7). Some of the data from this survey are displayed in tables 7 and 8. As demonstrated in these tables, a sizeable proportion of House members believe that financial disclosure re-

TABLE 8. House Members' Views of Earnings from Honoraria

Category of Response[a]	Percentage
Relax limit and expand earnings	6
Keep present rules	30
Tighten limit and reduce earnings	36
Totally eliminate honoraria	27
Not sure	2

Source: U.S. Congress, House 1977a, 917.

Note: One hundred and forty-six members surveyed.

[a]Question: "At the present time, the House rules permit Members to earn honoraria for speeches of up to $2000 each or an aggregate of $25,000 in any 1 year. How do you feel about the limitations on honoraria—should the limit be relaxed so that members could earn more than the present amounts permit, do you feel the limit ought to be kept as it is, do you feel that the limit ought to be tightened so as to reduce the amount of money members are permitted to earn from giving speeches, or do you feel that honoraria from speeches ought to be eliminated totally?" The percentage do not sum to 100 due to rounding.

quirements are too loose (63 percent) and favor tightening limits on honoraria (63 percent); only about 5–6 percent believe present limits on both are too stringent or need to be relaxed. In short, there seems to be considerable support for ethics codes that limit the exercise of discretion, at least discretion associated with financial gain.

What would drive rational, discretion-maximizing politicians to invoke legislative standards that restrict their capacities to exercise discretion? The motivating force is the desire to preserve their own "brand name capital," which represents the investments of legislators in developing and sustaining reputations with popular appeal. Popular contempt for legislators in general threatens a legislator's accumulated investment in his or her reputation. Brand names are what legislators depend upon to sustain the confidence and trust of constituents in the absence of personal contact, ensuring discretion in Washington and minimizing the demand for monitoring on the part of voters. Damage to the reputation of legislators in general could affect constituents' trust in their *own* representative, thereby depreciating brand name capital and subjecting the incumbent to more scrutiny by constituents and information gatherers. Therefore, it behooves incumbents to shield themselves and their own brand names from spillover effects—guilt by association. In short, the unethical behavior of even a few legislators creates externalities (external costs) for all who serve in Congress; one economic solution to the existence of externalities is for government (the legislature) to impose a remedy.

In order to protect their own discretion, legislators restricted it. Legislators guarantee themselves a large area of discretion by assuring constituents that they will not take *financial advantage* of them (or of their position as members of Congress); this assurance is legislated to ensure its durability. Thus, ethics laws can be viewed as consumer protection laws or product assurances (warranties).

It should be acknowledged that legislators do not normally take preventive actions to ensure the sanctity of their collective brand name. Most legislative efforts to establish ethical standards of conduct were precipitated by rather bizarre and obvious acts of wrongdoing. Generally, and throughout most of its history, Congress has been reluctant to establish formal, institutionally based rules of conduct for its members, and whenever possible, congressional majorities have chosen to administer the lesser of available punishments.

Before 1870, most of the censure proceedings (severe reprimands by a member's fellow legislators) in the House dealt with violent actions toward other legislators: assaults on other representatives accounted for five of the eighteen proceedings, with another seven proceedings associated with insults and offensive utterances. Clearly, corruption seemed to be a less-regarded evil. Between 1870 and 1876, however, six of the seven censure proceedings dealt with corruption. In short, corruption may not have been an important concern for an institution just trying to keep people civil, but by 1876, concern over corruption was evident. Still, it wasn't until 1968 that action to curb financial discretion finally became the ethical standard.

The first formal code of ethical conduct for House members was a result of the public and legislative outcry over the flamboyant behavior of Congressman Adam Clayton Powell (D—New York). Powell had already developed a history of legal problems including tax-evasion charges during his two decades in the House, but matters seemed to come to a boil when he was removed from his chairmanship of the Education and Labor Committee because of his cavalier disregard for his legislative responsibilities and long absences from Capitol Hill. Further investigation revealed that Powell had taken pleasure trips at the government's expense and paid his wife a salary even though she lived in Puerto Rico and never performed any office duties.

The speed with which Congress has moved in this area is rather remarkable when one considers the lack of incentives associated with either reprimanding colleagues or constraining members' own future discretion. Granted, it took until 1968 to get any kind of ethical code in place, but the trend in purging the institution of its most corrupt members is definitely heading upward: between 1941 and 1968, nine of the House members charged with criminal action were either indicted or sentenced; between 1969 and 1977, after the first ethics code and before the 1977 changes brought about by the Obey Commission, sixteen legislators were indicted; and between 1978 and 1987, fifteen more legislators faced the same fate.[2] In short, over 75 percent of the members of Congress indicted or sentenced for criminal action relating to fraud or corruption (not sexual misconduct) have faced prosecution since the passage of the first ethics code in 1968. This speed, to reiterate, has been brought about by some rather sensational cases of misconduct by members, such as Wayne Hayes, who was alleged to have hired secretary Elizabeth Ray on the public payroll of the House Administration Committee in return for sexual favors. In a very real sense, as bizarre expressions of legislator discretion were exposed, more constituents began to question the integrity of incumbent legislators; this, in turn, led to greater demand (on the part of voters) for *quality assurances*.[3]

Ethics laws provide some of the constraints that keep discretion-maximizing politicians from exploiting the institution to the point that it

---

2. These figures are compiled from *Congressional Ethics* (Congressional Quarterly 1982) and various volumes of the *Congressional Quarterly Almanac*.

3. A similar proposition is developed by Benjamin Klein and Keith B. Leffler (1981) in discussing the value of brand names in informing consumers of product quality: "The greater is the cost to consumers of obtaining deceptively low quality, the greater will be the demand for quality assurance" (632).

damages the reputations of all those involved. In economic terms, legislators want to preserve the reputations of their products—themselves—and the investments they have made in these reputations over time. Moreover, a legislator's untarnished brand name leads constituents to heavily discount perceptions of legislator shirking. One reason incumbency serves as an electoral advantage is because of the legislators' built-in reputations for helping constituents and supplying district services; but if incumbents can't be trusted, voters may heavily discount their promises to faithfully serve constituency interests and avoid shirking. At the very least, a damaged reputation is almost certain to intensify monitoring activities by information gatherers, voters, and potential candidates. In sum, ethics codes enable incumbents to preserve their brand names and thereby avoid monitoring activities that might severely limit the exercise of discretion within Congress.[4]

Restrictive Rules

The legislative agenda can be viewed as a nonexclusive resource, or "common pool." A nonexclusive resource, such as a common grazing land or a pool of oil extending under the property of several landowners, allows unrestricted access by any of its owners (Cheung 1970). If each owner is left to his or her own devices, the resource will be overutilized, rendering it useless to all. For example, when grazing ground is owned in common, all individuals have an incentive to allow their herds to graze as intensively as possible. The rationale is simple: grass not taken by one owner's herd will be consumed by other herds. As a result, the land is overgrazed and ends up being less productive for everyone. One solution to this problem is to allocate property rights so that each owner has an incentive to maximize the productivity of his or her land by not overgrazing.

---

4. There is probably another reason why legislators take measures to protect their brand names: brand names represent salvageable capital. In the market, brand names are considered nonsalvageable capital since there is no way for a firm to recoup its investments in promoting and polishing its brand name in uses outside the firm—these are sunk costs that are nonrecoverable. A legislator's brand name, in contrast, is at least partially salvageable. Respected politicians gain entry to postemployment opportunities often denied the disreputable, such as partnerships in prestigious law firms. The highly respected have more markets in which to sell their services. Perhaps more importantly, unflattering reputations may signal to potential purchasers of a legislator's postelective office services that he or she is a poor contractual risk because of some penchant for opportunism. Only industries that benefited from the actions of an opportunistic public official are likely to provide the politician with postelective office opportunities, but even these industries will be forced to pay "price premiums" and/or incur monitoring costs to assure contractual performance (Klein and Leffler 1981; Alchian and Demsetz 1972). If so, such industries will incorporate these costs into the compensation paid those with poor reputations, thereby reducing their earnings compared to more reputable legislators.

The legislative agenda suffers from the same problem: legislators are free to amend legislation, as long as their amendments are germane to the legislation and do not violate parliamentary rules. Discretion-maximizing legislators have strong incentives to use the amendment process to expand their influence over the making of public policy. Granted, the chances of noncommittee members amending committee legislation are not encouraging, but even if the chances of passage are slim, discretion-maximizing legislators reason that it is better to clog the agenda with doubtful amendments than not to try to inject their views into the formation of public policies.

The solution to this problem is similar to that of the overutilization of grazing land: assignment of property rights. The committee system can be viewed as an institutional arrangement that allocates access to the legislative agenda, making more efficient and productive the time and resources of legislators (Shepsle 1978; Holcombe and Parker 1991). The committee system, as mentioned earlier, subdivides the legislative agenda into smaller areas, corresponding to the jurisdictions of committees, and grants each committee exclusive rights to produce (and alter) legislation in that area.

This right loses its value if committee products are successfully amended on the floor, however. Even if a committee's legislation is not successfully amended, the time and resources taken to defeat amendments by noncommittee members reduce the efficiency and productivity of the legislature. It seems imperative, therefore, that party leaders take action to prevent members from using the legislative agenda as a vehicle for expanding their influence over legislation. Not only does amending activity devalue the property rights associated with committee membership but it also diminishes the efficiency and productivity of the legislature.

Legislative reorganization acts (the most recent in 1970) and the change in product advertising that began in the mid-1960s expanded legislator discretion, and offering amendments on the floor of the House seems like a natural outlet for such discretion. This may explain why amending activity, like discretion, has expanded in the House during recent decades. From the Eighty-fourth (1955–56) to the Ninety-second Congress (1971–72), amending activity increased in the House, reaching a plateau in the late 1960s. The Ninety-third Congress (1973–74) marked an explosion in amending activity, eventually reaching a peak in the Ninety-fifth Congress (1977–78), but from the Ninety-seventh Congress (1981–82) through the Ninety-ninth Congress (1985–86), amending activity diminished (Smith 1989, 16). Similarly, the proportion of legislative measures considered on the floor and subjected to amendment increased almost monotonically during the late 1950s and 1960s, before peaking during the mid-1970s and receding (Smith 1989, 17–18). Special rules to House legislation in the late 1980s helped to restrict and reduce this surge in amending activity:

By the 99th Congress (1985–86), nearly half of all special rules restricted amending activity in some way, up from just over 15 percent in the 94th (1975–76) and about 31 percent in the 96th (1979–80). . . . For the top layer of key vote measures, over 86 percent were subject to a restrictive rule in the 99th Congress, compared with just 36 percent in the 94th and 48 percent in the 96th. By the start of the 100th Congress (1987–88), one could safely assume that the most important, controversial measures would be taken to the floor under a rule that limited and ordered floor amendments in some fashion. (Smith 1989, 74)

Restrictive provisions typically prohibit all amendments except (1) those specifically identified or enumerated by a (House) rule, (2) all amendments to certain portions of the measure, or (3) those on certain topics in the legislation. The growth in such restrictive rules is rather startling: open rules to legislation (no limitations on amendments) accounted for 84.3 percent of the rules in the Ninety-fourth Congress (1975–76), but the number declined to 55.4 percent in the Ninety-ninth Congress (1985–86); conversely, the percentage of restrictive rules climbed from 11.3 percent to 33.7 percent during the same period. On measures associated with key votes, the number of restrictive rules rose from 31.8 percent in the Ninety-fourth Congress to 72.7 percent in the Ninety-ninth Congress (Bach and Smith 1988, 57).

While the growth of restrictive rules might be viewed as a natural response by the majority party in Congress to a growing Republican trend in the country during the 1980s, there are other, more practical reasons for a discretion-maximizing legislature to permit its leaders to constrain members' discretion. Increased use of floor amendments is not just a bother to party leaders but also a nuisance for all members. Controversial bills, which always consume lots of time, take up even more valuable agenda time when they are required to withstand onslaughts of floor amendments. Therefore, in order to keep their investments in their committees safe and valuable, and to increase the efficiency of the legislative process, which benefits all members, legislators allowed their party leaders to limit the exercise of discretion on the floor of the House. As a result, more legislative initiatives could receive congressional attention, especially committee products. Discretion-maximizing legislators may have lost some influence, but they could gain solace from knowing that their monopoly over a segment of the legislative agenda was once again intact.

Nonpecuniary Returns

Constraints placed on discretion make nonpecuniary benefits quite attractive. There are a number of reasons why nonpecuniary gains are appealing to legislators. Legislators are, of course, more interested in monetary gain since money can be traded in more markets than can nonpecuniary gains. But limitations placed on discretion, especially financial discretion, have led members of Congress to exploit the nonpecuniary benefits available to them. Nonpecuniary benefits are attractive because Congress has refused to severely regulate most nonpecuniary benefits; nonpecuniary benefits are easy to conceal or, in any event, such benefits are difficult to monitor; finally, nonpecuniary benefits may be more easily justified than monetary benefits, such as salary increases. As a result, there are more attempts today to exploit these benefits than in the past.

The trend in foreign travel is suggestive of the emphasis on nonpecuniary benefits: there is more foreign travel, with more members taking such travel. Based on reports filed by congressional committees detailing foreign travel (published in the *Congressional Record*), the mean number of foreign trips taken between 1968 and the sweeping ethics reform package in 1977 was 1.55, and the mean number of House members accounting for such travel during this period was 177. After 1977, the mean number of foreign trips increased to 1.70, and the mean number of legislators responsible for these trips was 213 (1978–87). In the Congresses following the passage of the 1977 ethics reforms (1979–86), an average of 749 trips were taken, as compared to a mean of 633 trips for the Congresses preceding the Ninety-sixth (the Ninety-second to Ninety-fifth Congress).[5] Clearly, foreign travel has gained attrac-

---

5. The figures from which these generalizations are drawn are as follows:

Years	Mean number of Trips	Legislators
1968	1.44	159
1971	1.77	209
1972	1.42	187
1974	1.53	154
1975	1.84	261
1976	1.40	109
1977	1.46	158
1978	1.77	226
1979	1.71	205
1980	1.57	216
1981	1.49	158
1982	1.71	255
1983	1.77	187
1984	2.00	255
1985	1.51	170
1986	1.86	257
1987	1.60	199

This is based on reports published in the *Congressional Record* (U.S. Government Printing Office). No reports are available for 1969, 1970, and 1973.

tiveness, and the restrictions placed on financial gain may have enhanced the attractiveness of this nonpecuniary benefit. The absence of congressional controls on foreign travel make junketing an inviting target for the exercise of legislator discretion.

Conclusion

Diligent personal attention to constituency affairs helps increase the ability of legislators to maneuver and exercise discretion in Washington. Neither the financial costs associated with constituency service, nor the declining value of an overproduced product, operate to constrain the efforts of legislators to cultivate their constituencies. Constituency services are highly subsidized by the government, and few voters believe that adequate substitutes can be found for their member's service to constituents. Congress has also attempted to reduce the opportunity costs associated with constituency service by increasing staff and modifying the legislative schedule to accommodate the demands of its members. Despite these efforts, constituency service imposes a burden on legislators because the personal attention that it requires (e.g., visits to the constituency) reduces the time that legislators can devote to the pursuit of private goals in Washington. This is a natural result of the zero-sum nature of personal attention: for instance, spending time visiting with constituents in the district or state reduces the time available for pursuing personal interests in Washington. Thus, the opportunity costs associated with personal attention to constituency affairs set limits on the amount of time legislators spend cultivating constituents and thereby enhancing their discretion. Legislators will only cultivate their districts until that effort handicaps their pursuit of their own private interests—the exercise of discretion.

The exercise of discretion can pose problems for a political institution. First, if some legislators use their freedom from monitoring to engage in unethical behavior, all members incur some cost if such misconduct is uncovered. The external effects or "fall-out" resulting from exposés of congressional malfeasance damage the images of all who serve in Congress, depreciating the over-time investments that members have made in their reputations. Second, discretion in policy making may ultimately result in a crowded legislative agenda, as legislators exploit the legislative process for their own aims. All members of Congress suffer from a congested legislative agenda because it reduces the probability that their pet bills will receive adequate attention in the legislative process. These problems are not merely hypothetical but have created real dilemmas for members of Congress: legislators can avoid the adverse effects stemming from the ethical transgressions of others, and the overuse of the legislative agenda, only by constraining their own exercise of discretion. The benefits resulting from constraining the capacity of discretion-maximizing legislators to engage in questionable ethical practices, and to inject their personal views into a whole range of legislative issues, were sufficiently widespread to induce members to accept rules restricting their conduct inside and outside of Congress, and limiting their ability to amend legislation. In sum, the opportunity costs attached to the personal cultivation of constituents, and the institutional rules that mark the legislative process, constrain the discretion-maximizing behavior of legislators.

CHAPTER 6

Some Concluding Observations on Discretion-Maximizing Behavior in Legislatures

Summary of Arguments: A Theory of Discretion-Maximization in Legislatures

It is important at this point to weave together the strands of the arguments that define my theory of discretion-maximization in legislatures. The basic premise is that barriers to entry into legislatures create vote surpluses that legislators spend with discretion. There are a variety of barriers to entry. For instance, legal restrictions prohibit some from seeking office. In earlier decades, when travel between legislators' districts and Washington was far more hazardous than today, the length of the legislative session may have restricted some who could not risk the time away from their primary occupations.[1] Farmers, for example, may have suffered from the lengthening of legislative sessions because it interfered with the cycles in planting and harvesting so important to their basic livelihood. The low salaries offered in some state legislatures may deter qualified candidates from seeking office; as barriers to entry were established, however, the need to keep legislative salaries low disappeared. Electoral realignments function as natural barriers to entry that create pockets of electoral safety.

There are also institutionally contrived barriers to entry that incumbents have exploited.[2] Monopolies over legislation and bureaucratic fix-it services serve as barriers to entry because of the control they give incumbents over resources essential for the survival and benefit of groups and constituents. As members of the cartel that produces legislation, incumbents can bestow benefits through the laws passed by the legislature; these benefits endear groups and voters to incumbents and thereby deter qualified candidates from challenging widely esteemed incumbents. Similarly, the monopoly over bu-

---

1. I have analyzed the effects of the length of the session on the expansion of discretion, but the relationship never achieved statistical significance in any of the equations examined.

2. Nelson Polsby (1985) suggests that the "contested election process" has evolved to favor incumbents. If correct, such a procedure also constitutes a barrier to entry.

reaucratic favors enables incumbents to promote the best interests of those dependent upon federal programs.

There are numerous examples of how legislators have intervened to influence bureaucratic decisions to the benefit of constituents. Perhaps the most notable relate to the efforts of representatives and senators to keep military bases open through legislative and extralegislative methods. For instance, the military construction authorization of FY 1980 (a conference report) ensured that five military bases that had been singled out by the Department of Defense (DOD) to be closed would remain open; similarly, Senator Daniel Inouye (D—Hawaii) inserted a section into the FY 1983 supplemental appropriations bill that prohibited DOD from disposing of any part of Fort DeRussy, Hawaii, a seventy-three-acre facility with 147 personnel (Fitzgerald and Lipson 1984, 19–21). Senator Mack Mattingly (D—Georgia) placed language in appropriations legislation to prevent the forest service from consolidating and closing the Oconee ranger district in Georgia; Senator Robert Byrd (D—West Virginia) took a similar action to prevent Amtrak (a federally funded national railroad corporation) from terminating a money-losing long-distance passenger line through West Virginia (Fitzgerald and Lipson 1984). Many times, however, legislators' phone calls, visits, political exchanges, and exploitation of personal relationships influence bureaucratic decisions without their resorting to legislative imperatives.

Even open competition for scarce federal grant money is subject to congressional influence. For example, by inserting language into legislation to prevent open competition for education grants, limiting funding to institutions already receiving grants, senators have ensured continued funding in their states. Senators Harrison Schmitt (R—New Mexico) and Robert Stafford (R—Vermont) followed this strategy by singling out colleges with strong Hispanic and native American enrollments for special assistance, diverting $5.3 million out of $10 million added to the program to institutions almost exclusively in New Mexico and Vermont (Fitzgerald and Lipson 1984, 68).

Personal contacts within the legislature, control over agency budgets, and the use of legislative directives place incumbents in a position to affect bureaucratic decisions to the benefit of constituents. In short, it is quite easy for incumbents to ingratiate themselves to district interests as a result of their membership in the legislative cartel. (I refer to Congress as a legislative cartel because both are supported by the same set of forces: agreements among members to limit entry and to segment output [political favors and legislation] among markets or, in the case of legislatures, districts.)

Office perquisites are legislature-sponsored subsidies that also raise barriers to entry by escalating the costs of campaigning against incumbents, who control enormous resources that enable them to campaign on a daily basis. Many of these perks are direct subsidies for electioneering, such as staff and office allowances, though they also serve other more justifiable ends (e.g., communicating with constituents and keeping voters informed).

Campaign war chests, commonly accumulated by incumbents, create a form of "excess capacity"—a means of blocking the entry of new competitors. Economists define excess capacity as a situation where the output actually produced is less than the level of output that would minimize average total cost; simply put, it is the unused capacity for the scale of a plant that a firm has constructed. This signals potential competitors considering entry that those holding such an excess capacity can quickly increase production and thereby lower prices if competition threatens. This effectively deters entry.

Legislators create similar conditions by accumulating large campaign war chests months prior to an election from the surpluses created by past successful campaigns and nonelection year fund-raising. This deters challengers from contesting the reelection of incumbents because of the incumbents' overwhelming edge in campaign funds, which enables incumbents to quickly raise the costs to those contesting their reelections. A large reservoir of campaign funds scares off potential opposition who fear that any credible challenge to a well-financed incumbent will be unusually costly. While lavish spending by an incumbent does not necessitate a dollar-for-dollar battle, efforts to counter such spending normally escalate the campaign costs incurred by congressional challengers. Such cost considerations may deter quality candidates from contesting the reelection of entrenched incumbents. This may be one reason why incumbents do not conceal their off-year activities to raise campaign funds and do not appear to resent the media's attention to the size of their campaign coffers.

It can be inferred from the persistence of barriers to entry that legislators need not worry very much about reelection. Some astute congressional observers (see, for example, Mann 1978) have argued that incumbents are less complacent about their electoral safety than would be expected from the magnitude of their electoral resources and margins. The argument is often made that the diligent efforts of incumbents to win reelection is evidence of this "running scared" mentality. While I would not dispute the fact that incumbents exert considerable effort to win reelection, I do challenge the conclusion that the intensity of their reelection activities is indicative of a fear of losing reelection. For some, intense campaigning may indeed reflect electoral insecurity, but I suspect that for the vast majority such activity is designed to create large vote surpluses that expand their capacities to safely exercise discretion in Washington. In sum, incumbents expend considerable effort in their reelection contests, but they do not do so because of a fear of losing reelection; rather, the effort is directed at running up large reelection majorities to sustain discretionary actions in Washington.

Despite the accumulation of vote surpluses, incumbents were unlikely to spend them with discretion until rules could be established to guarantee that the investment and exercise of discretion would be beyond the reach of their party leaders. Only with the establishment of such guarantees—durable legislative rules guaranteeing and protecting the exercise of discretion—were members inclined to expand existing levels of discretion. But why would legislative leaders want to support the discretionary actions of their party members since such actions reduce party cohesion and loyalty?

Party leaders function as residual claimants who retain any chits not needed to pass legislation. These favors are obtained from other legislators, groups, presidents, and voters in return for the passage of legislation. Party leaders function as intermediaries in the legislative exchanges necessary to pass legislation. Their ability to clear the market and produce legislation earns them IOU's that they can, in turn, spend at their own discretion. In short, party leaders have every incentive to keep the legislature as productive as possible since their gains are largely dependent upon the productivity of the legislature.[3] The production of legislation is not, of course, all gain for party leaders; there are a number of costs involved in clearing the market. One of the major costs legislative leaders incur in clearing the market is the cost of transacting the agreements.

A major transaction cost occurs as leaders make deals with other party members, normally those who speak for large collectivities or blocs. Committee leaders fall into the category of party members that party leaders *must* negotiate with to ensure the passage of legislation. The costs of such negotiations will be a function of the number of committee leaders that party leaders include in their negotiations, assuming that the time involved is equivalent. Party leaders can minimize these costs, and gain a greater return from their intermediary efforts, by reducing the number of committees, and therefore committee leaders, that they must deal with in producing legislation. This logic favors a few large-sized committees, but the fear of members shirking due to the large size of these few committees restrains leaders from consolidating the existing committees into a few large ones. Party leaders might be able to overcome the problems associated with free riding and shirking in team-production situations by instilling a sense of team spirit or party loyalty, but such an effort is doomed to failure. Since voters show little loyalty to the political parties, how can leaders expect those elected to show any more respect for the parties?

Clearly, the major way that party leaders can ensure a productive legisla-

---

3. Robert McCormick and Robert D. Tollison (1979) suggest that the pay of party leaders is linked to the work load (productivity) of the legislature: the number of bills introduced is positively related to the additional yearly pay received by majority leaders in state legislatures above and beyond the normal pay of legislators.

ture is to create conditions that motivate legislators to be productive; then leaders can reap the benefits of the increased productivity through their positions as residual claimants. One way that members can be motivated to increase their productivity is by expanding their levels of discretion. For example, expanding legislator discretion by increasing the number of committee assignments held by members of Congress moves the legislature to a higher level of productivity. Therefore, with only a fixed number of legislators, and without increasing the number of committees, the productivity of the legislature could be increased.

Party leaders cannot *force* members to demand more committee assignments; to do so would only encourage shirking and impair the productivity that party leaders hope to realize. For these reasons, party leaders acquiesce and establish rules to protect the discretion of their members. Such rules, like the series of legislative reforms in Congress, protect major areas of member discretion: committee decision making and the power of individual committee members. Thus, the Legislative Reorganization Act of 1946 and of 1970 led many members to increase their investments in the committee system by assuming more committee assignments. The expansion of these investments (in committee assignments) enabled leaders to move the legislature to a higher level of productivity, increasing the output of laws and the returns to party leaders.

In addition to making the legislature more productive, the expansion of discretion made legislative life more attractive. As a consequence, careers in Congress lengthened; I suspect that the same phenomena is true of most legislatures. Legislatures, especially Congress, tend to attract people from some of the most successful and financially well-off strata in society. The attraction of legislative service for such individuals is the ability to exercise discretion, especially on issues about which they hold intense opinions. These are just the types of issues where vote surpluses are important since there is always the possibility that the legislator's exercise of discretion will offend, if not anger, many constituents. Without significant vote surpluses, politicians would be more constrained by the opinions of constituents and groups. Simply put, the exercise of discretion costs votes.

Summary of Empirical Findings

This analysis produces evidence that members accumulate committee assignments—expand their discretion—over time in response to the raising of barriers to entry, barriers that are partially a result of greater personal contact with constituents. The most important factors promoting the expansion of areas of committee discretion (committee assignments) were the two durable legislative reform bills: the Legislative Reorganization Act of 1946 and of

1970. Contrived barriers to entry, resulting from increased subsidies for personal advertising (represented by the ratio of days in recess to days in actual session) and legislative rules protecting the discretion of committee members explain 97 percent of the variation in the expansion of discretion in the House of Representatives.

Team spirit—party loyalty—is influenced by the subsequent fragmentation of victorious realignment coalitions inside Congress and by the expansion of discretion by individual party members. Both factors diminish team spirit and reduce party loyalty ($R^2 = .49$). The lack of party loyalty complicates the task for party leaders of keeping the legislature productive. Legislative productivity responds to the electoral safety of legislators: the more resources incumbents can invest in legislative pursuits rather than electioneering, the more effort they direct toward producing legislation. The expansion of discretion also increases productivity.

The monetary incentives for pursuing long congressional careers appear to be far less important to legislators than the expansion of discretion and the greater opportunities to shirk associated with large legislatures. In fact, the monetary incentives are statistically insignificant: neither the potential for rent extractions vis-à-vis the passage of private bills nor the growth in legislative salaries is strongly related to the growth in mean terms of congressional service. One reason why monetary incentives are rather insignificant in motivating congressional careerism is because most of the gains from legislative service can only be captured upon leaving office. In sum, the expansion of discretion appears to be a significant factor in the decline in party voting, the growth in careerism, and the productivity of Congress—major forces shaping Congress.

Some Testable Propositions

The model described and summarized in the preceding pages yields a number of interesting deductions. In the following I describe some of these propositions and how they correspond to my theory of discretion-maximization in legislatures.

PROPOSITION 1: *Legislators spend the vote surpluses created by barriers to entry by increasing discretionary behavior.*

Legislators take advantage of the existence of barriers to entry by seizing opportunities to expand their discretion. In fact, legislators contrive to create such barriers. As noted, the existence of barriers to entry reduces the threat of competition and enables legislators to give greater rein to their own predilections and preferences. Expressions of discretion can be found in legislators' displays of ideological or altruistic voting, pursuit of specific interests and causes, shirking (e.g., junketing), or lining their pockets with gold. The most electorally safe members have the greatest amount of discretion available for consumption.

PROPOSITION 2: *Barriers to entry motivate legislators to create rules and procedures to protect their discretionary actions from interference by party leaders.*

Legislators are unable to spend their vote surpluses, or they are unwilling to spend them, without assurance that they will not be spending their vote margins foolishly. This requires the establishment of durable rules to protect the exercise of discretion; only then will incumbents be sufficiently motivated through the reduction in electoral risk to increase existing levels of discretion. Party leaders might oppose such rules since they reduce their control, but the gains through increased productivity motivate leaders to accept and promote rules that ensure the rights of members to exercise discretion.

PROPOSITION 3: *Legislators seek to expand existing levels of discretion.*

The major assumption in the model is that legislators act as if they were trying to maximize their own discretion. I consider the expansion of discretion a major factor motivating the behavior of legislators. For instance, the expansion of discretion increases the attractiveness of legislative service more so than higher salaries or more private bills. Increases in committee assignments are just one aspect of the expansion of discretion; increased ideological voting or junketing are other.

PROPOSITION 4: *Legislators exploit nonpecuniary benefits.*

Members of Congress can be expected to exploit the use of the perks associated with the office because the exploitation of these perks is difficult to monitor and the use of these perks is easier to explain to voters than the monetary gains from office holding. For these reasons, nonpecuniary benefits hold quite an attraction. A corollary to this proposition is that discretionary behavior is most likely to occur where it is most difficult to monitor.

PROPOSITION 5: *The costs of monitoring the actions of legislators rise with the size of the legislature.*

As the size of a legislature increases, more shirking is likely to occur since metering and monitoring costs make shirking more difficult to detect. It is almost impossible in large legislatures to detect the individual contributions of members, and this anonymity can be exploited by legislators. Party leaders can control some shirking by expanding control mechanisms, such as assistant party leaders (e.g., whips in Congress); however, the imperfect nature of these control relationships and the many areas where discretion can be practiced and escape the notice of party leaders provide considerable opportunities for members in large legislatures to exercise discretion.

PROPOSITION 6: *The expansion of discretion increases legislative productivity.*

The expansion of discretion and its associated protections motivate members to expend considerable time and energy on legislative business. For instance, the protections accorded committees motivate members to invest more of their scarce resources in their committee careers and to expand those investments. As more time and energy is spent on legislative pursuits, and less time on electioneering (due to barriers to entry), the productivity of the legislature increases.

PROPOSITION 7: *The discretionary actions of leaders increase with the productivity of the legislature.*

Since party leaders earn returns from making deals that enhance the productivity of the legislature, we can expect leaders to exercise greater discretion as the productivity of the legislature increases. The returns, in the form of chits owed party leaders that are not subsequently used in market-clearing efforts, can be used with discretion by party leaders. This makes the influence of party leaders considerably greater than that of party members. Simply put, party leaders enjoy the fruits of their labors by calling in chits that enable them to give free expression to their *own* predilections and preferences, just like other discretion-maximizing legislators. The only difference is that the position of party leader enables him or her to accumulate favors that give that leader a far greater say and influence than other, if not all, party members. We often attribute the productivity of legislatures to the power of individual party leaders; the relationship, however, may flow in the opposite direction—productive legislatures make party leaders powerful.

PROPOSITION 8: *The expansion of discretion reduces party loyalty.*

Party loyalty requires that individual legislators subjugate their own opinions to the party consensus. Party positions, not individual preferences, must rule if party loyalty is to prevail. Discretion-maximizing legislators, however, view party loyalty as a constraining force on their entrepreneurial activities. Moreover, there is something of a domino theory associated with the expansion of discretion—it motivates imitation by other party members. When members see others exercising discretion without trepidation, and escaping any sort of rebuke by party leaders, the motivations to follow the party line diminish rapidly. This reduces party loyalty. I provide some empirical evidence that the expansion of discretion reduced party voting in the House of Representatives during the past one hundred years.

PROPOSITION 9: *The ability to exercise discretion is an attractive feature of legislative service.*

It is not exactly clear what makes legislative service attractive to an electorally motivated membership; reelection, itself, does not seem sufficiently valuable for members to establish long careers in Congress, especially given present constraints on financial gain that limit rent extractions. In fact, most incumbent legislators probably benefit more when they *leave* office than while *serving in* office. As I demonstrate, the expansion of discretion seems central to longevity in office, more so than even electoral safety. For a membership composed of some of the richest and most successful men and women in society, neither money nor reelection can compete with the utility derived from influencing the making of public policy. Certainly the exercise of discretion can lead to increases in salary, rent extractions, and shirking, but even after I have statistically controlled for these expressions of discretion, the increase in policy-making influence (the expansion of committee assignments) still remains one of the strongest factors promoting careerism in the House. I expect that expressions of discretion that reflect policymaker independence motivate members to seek and remain in office.

PROPOSITION 10: *Personal contacts with constituents—incumbent advertising—increase vote surpluses and discretion.*

The personal contacts that legislators have with their constituents promote vote surpluses by increasing the demand for the incumbents' district services, reducing the elasticity of that demand, and promoting voter trust. Members of Congress use their personal contacts with constituents to differentiate their products (themselves) from all existing and potential competitors for their offices. This serves to increase voters' support and ensures reliable cores of supporters. Personal contacts solidify voter coalitions by promoting trusting attitudes toward incumbents (Fenno 1978; Parker and Parker 1989); such attitudes provide incumbents with critical leeway to maneuver in Washington and reduce the incentives for constituents to monitor the behavior of their legislators. Institutional arrangements that force representatives to stand for reelection every two years but allow senators a longer breathing spell guarantee higher levels of discretion for senators. However, the greater personal contacts of representatives with their constituents provide them with better opportunities to create large, electorally safe coalitions that tolerate high levels of legislator discretion (Parker 1986).

It seems quite possible that many of the propositions regarding the evolution of Congress could be applied to state legislatures. We might expect to see, for instance, that the most-productive legislatures are associated with decentralized decision-making processes that permit legislators greater latitude than they might enjoy in more centralized party structures. Indeed, there is some empirical evidence to support this premise. Wayne Francis has noted that centralized leadership structures in state legislatures reduce the legislative output of these states (1989, 63). Francis also presents evidence suggesting that committees may be a good place to shirk: the larger the committees in state legislatures, the lower the level of membership attendance (1989, 117–18). The productivity of state legislatures may also be related to party loyalty in the sense that such team spirit reduces shirking and enhances the efficiency of the legislative process. Similarly, the decline in the powers of centralized party leaders in state legislatures and the concomitant increase in the autonomy of legislative committees may be a rational exchange designed to increase the productivity of state legislatures: party leaders gain from keeping the legislature productive while members reap the benefits from increased discretion and the assurance that the exercise of discretion will be protected. In short, there is some reason to believe that discretion-maximization may go beyond Washington and also affect the behavior of state legislators.[4]

Discretion in the Postreform Congress

Several recent changes in Congress have given a new look to the institution. Three important attributes of the postreform Congress are particularly important since they reflect significant changes in how Congress does its business. First, there has been an increase in restrictive rules that prohibit certain actions on the floor of Congress (chap. 5). Restrictive rules may constrain decision making on the floor of the House and therefore reduce expressions of discretion, but they also strengthen the monopoly power of committees over

---

4. There are other propositions related to the assumption of discretion-maximization but not easily deduced from the theory. For instance, discretion probably increases with seniority: older members exercise more discretion than younger legislators because they are more likely to discount future returns from congressional service or to discount these returns at a higher rate. For some empirical evidence supporting this proposition, see Davis and Porter 1989.

legislation falling into their jurisdictions. In fact, the use of restrictive rules may have been necessary to preserve the monopoly power of committees since the increased use of the floor to fashion legislation challenged the dominance of the committee system. Restrictive rules sustain that primacy.

Second, there has been an increase in the number of legislative measures that are multiply referred. This means that more committees get a shot at each piece of legislation. In a very real sense, this compromises the monopoly power of committees by forcing committee products to survive the scrutiny of other committees. On the other hand, multiple referrals expand the policy influence over the legislative agenda exercised by individual members by permitting them influence over a broader range of legislation.

Finally, legislative leaders in the postreform Congress are far more active in legislative matters than in the past. Does this mean that the discretion of members is on the wane? I think not. The increase in legislative leadership is basically directed at the management of the legislative schedule. The efficient operation of the schedule not only benefits leaders by increasing the returns they can capture through increased production but it also benefits individual members who have a stake in the efficient operation of the legislative process. For instance, rules designed to limit dilatory actions benefit legislators who seek gains from keeping the legislature productive and passing their pet bills. Efficiency also means a more-productive usage of time—the scarcest of all commodities for legislators.

In conclusion, recent developments do not appear to significantly constrain the discretion of legislators. If anything, these developments seem quite in line with what one might expect of legislators seeking to maximize their own discretion.

Representation of Constituency Opinion

The lack of electoral restraints leads to questions about the representation of constituency opinion. In short, in the absence of an electoral constraint, how does representation occur in a discretion-maximizing legislature? In a competitive situation, we might expect the representation of constituency opinion to occur because of the fear of being ousted by an opponent who better represents that opinion. The evidence of the impact of electoral margins on candidates' opinions has failed to produce such a relationship, but it seems that representation would suffer where safety was the general rule. This may not be necessarily true, however, since there is evidence that electorally safe incumbents are more in tune with their constituents than marginally elected legislators (Miller 1964)! There are a number of characteristics associated with electoral safety, such as the homogeneity of the district and the accuracy of the perceptions of district opinion by longtime members of Congress, so it is difficult to attribute better representation merely to electoral safety. Still, the accepted view that barriers to entry prevent the representation of *constituency opinion* is not without caveats.

Representation in a discretion-maximizing legislature is likely to be both collective and virtual. The dyadic perspective on representation views representation almost exclusively in terms of a particular legislator and the constituency that elected that legislator; conversely, representation can be thought of in terms of institutions collectively representing a society or people. Thus, the question under a system of collective representation is not so much whether or not each member of Congress represents his or her constituency, but whether or not Congress as an institution represents the American people. In this view, a legislature is a group of individuals collectively representing the people as a whole:

> The purpose of the legislature is to create an accurate reflection of the community; misrepresentation occurs when the diverse interests and opinions of the political community are excluded from debate. A particular legislator . . . was not a delegate for those particular people who chose him or her, but all the legislators taken collectively would act as if all the people themselves were acting since they were a reflection of the whole. (Weissberg 1978, 536–37)

That is, the institution can represent the collective interests in society without a dyadic correspondence between the opinions of the legislator and those of his or her constituents. "If individual legislators are 'free' to deviate from district opinion it is likely that the deviations will approach normality and the institution as a whole will be more representative of national opinion than the average legislator is representative of district opinion" (Weissberg 1978, 547). In short, it may be impossible for one legislator to accurately represent 500,000 constituents, but it is far more reasonable to expect 435 legislators to represent the opinion of 220 million citizens with a higher degree of accuracy.

In addition to representing societal opinion, legislators represent constituency opinion because they have internalized the values and attitudes within the communities they represent; hence, as they express their own attitudes and values, they are also expressing the consensus within their own communities (virtual representation). Residence requirements and plain good political sense force successful legislators to live and grow up in the districts they represent, and most can boast of long histories of community attachment and involvement. This means that most legislators have been socialized to the dominant values within their communities, and these internalized values become the legislators own values without much change in subsequent years. Thus, when legislators are expressing their own views and exercising discretion, they are also expressing the views that are dominant within their districts without explicitly attempting to do so. "The constituency orientations are an integral part of his [the incumbent's] being. They are operative in his personal political attitudes, in his cognition of the political environment, and in his views on a variety of non-political matters, some of which become intertwined with his politics" (Clausen 1973, 132).

In sum, representation does occur within a discretion-maximizing legislature because the collective attitudes within society are represented along with those of constituents. The process is not, however, one of dyadic correspondence; rather, it is conditioned by probabilities and the inculcation of community attitudes by long-term residents. This form of representation is unlikely to satisfy many, but it is the best we can expect from a legislature dominated by discretion-maximizing politicians.[5]

Conclusion

One final question remains: can the patterns of behavior that Polsby and Dodd describe as illustrating the dynamics of their individual theories be explained by my theory of discretion-maximization? The growth in congressional careers, perquisites of office, universalistic rules, House expenditures, and the decline in member turnover can be described in terms of the expansion of discretion. As pointed out, the growth in careers is a direct result of the expansion of discretion, which increased the attractiveness of a congressional career. The growth in office perquisites and the decline in turnover are related to the raising of barriers to entry—a major precondition for the expansion of discretion. The emergence of universalistic rules is a result of the need for party leaders to guarantee legislators the security of their career investments in order to increase the productivity of the legislature; such rules encourage the expansion of discretion. Finally, the growth in House expenditures is closely related to the expansion of discretion $(r > .9)$.

Dodd's cyclical theory (1985) of decentralization-centralization is also consistent with elements of my theory. The decentralization cycle corresponds to the expansion of discretion—policymaker independence. The centralization cycle occurs when members encourage their leaders to take action to prevent the outgrowth of discretion from devaluing the property rights associated with committee membership, and reducing the efficiency of the legislative process—a detriment to the productive efforts of discretion-maximizing legislators. This is not to argue that the theory of discretion-maximization

---

5. Despite the existence of barriers to entry, members of Congress do not ignore constituency opinion entirely. In fact, there is evidence that some discretionary behavior decreases as elections approach (Kalt and Zupan 1984; Thomas 1985).

replaces these existing theories, but that discretion-maximization can account for the same behavior so eloquently explained by past theories of congressional evolution.

In conclusion, discretion-maximizing legislatures are valuable in producing legislation and ensuring the attractiveness of the job. There is another benefit of a discretion-maximizing legislature: the promotion and passage of public interest legislation. The exercise of discretion reflects the type of leeway necessary to pass legislation that serves the best interests of society, rather than the narrow self-interest of constituents. Legislators who neither have to worry about reelection nor devote all of their energies and resources to that end can ignore the self-interests of constituents and support public-spirited legislation. This may be the mechanism through which public interest or controversial legislation (e.g., tax reform) stays alive on the legislative agenda and, when conditions permit, is passed. Only a discretion-maximizing legislature, rather than a reelection-motivated one, is willing and prepared to incur the cost of angering voters by pursuing altruistic outcomes instead of the self-interests of constituents.

While discretion-maximization might ultimately lead to the decay of the legislature as a policy-making force, durable rules and institutional constraints have prevented this from occurring. Furthermore, while discretion-maximizing legislators might line their pockets with gold, monetary incentives (or gains) are rather insignificant factors in motivating long congressional tenure. Still, discretion-maximization neither promotes nor ensures the representation of constituency opinion in the legislature.

References

Alchian, Armen A., and Harold Demsetz. 1972. "Production, Information Costs, and Economic Organization." *American Economic Review*, December, 777–95.

Alford, John, and David W. Brady. 1988. *Partisan and Incumbent Advantage in U.S. House Elections, 1846–1986*. Working Paper Series, Center for the Study of Institutions and Values, no. 11. Houston: Rice University.

Arnold, R. Douglas. 1979. *Congress and the Bureaucracy: A Theory of Influence*. New Haven, Conn.: Yale University Press.

Arrow, Kenneth. 1970. *Essays in the Theory of Risk-Bearing*. Amsterdam: North-Holland Publishing Company.

Asher, Herbert B., and Herbert F. Weisberg. 1978. "Voting Change in Congress: Some Dynamic Perspectives on an Evolutionary Process." *American Journal of Political Science*, May, 391–425.

Bach, Stanley, and Steven S. Smith. 1988. *Managing Uncertainty in the House of Representatives*. Washington, D.C.: Brookings Institution.

Baker, Richard Allan. 1985. "The History of Congressional Ethics." in *Representation and Responsibility*, edited by Bruce Jennings and Daniel Callahan, 3–27. New York: Plenum Press.

Berry, Jeffrey. 1984. *The Interest Group Society*. Boston: Little, Brown.

Brady, David W. 1988. *Critical Elections and Congressional Policy Making*. Stanford, Calif.: Stanford University Press.

Brady, David W., and Charles S. Bullock III. 1980. "Is There a Conservative Coalition in the House?" *Journal of Politics*, May, 549–59.

Brady, David W., and Naomi Lynn. 1973. "Switched-Seat Congressional Districts: Their Effect on Party Voting and Public Policy." *American Journal of Political Science*, August, 528–43.

Brady, David W., Joseph Cooper, and Patricia Hurley. 1979. "The Decline of Party in the U.S. House of Representatives, 1887–1968." *Legislative Studies Quarterly*, August, 381–406.

Brookshire, Robert G., and Dean F. Duncan III. 1983. "Congressional Career Patterns and Party Systems." *Legislative Studies Quarterly*, February, 65–78.

Buchanan, James M., and Gordon Tullock. 1962. *The Calculus of Consent*. Ann Arbor: University of Michigan Press.

Calvert, Randall B., and John A. Ferejohn. 1983. "Coattail Voting in Recent Presidential Elections." *American Political Science Review*, June, 407–19.

Campbell, Angus, Phillip E. Converse, Warren E. Miller, and Donald E. Stokes, eds. 1966. *Elections and the Political Order*. New York: John Wiley.

Caves, Richard. 1977. *American Industry: Structure, Conduct, Performance*. Englewood Cliffs, N.J.: Prentice-Hall.

Cheung, Steven N. S. 1970. "The Structure of a Contract and the Theory of a Non-Exclusive Resource." *Journal of Law and Economics*, April, 49–70.

Clausen, Aage. 1973. *How Congressmen Decide*. New York: St. Martin's Press.

Congressional Quarterly. 1971–1989. *Congressional Quarterly Almanac*, vols. 26–44.

Congressional Quarterly. 1982. *Congressional Ethics*. 2d ed. Washington, D.C.: Congressional Quarterly.

Cooper, Joseph, and David W. Brady. 1981. "Institutional Context and Leadership Style: The House from Cannon to Rayburn." *American Political Science Review*, June, 411–25.

Cover, Albert D. 1977. "One Good Term Deserves Another: The Advantage of Incumbency in Congressional Elections." *American Journal of Political Science*, August, 523–42.

Crain, W. Mark, Donald R. Leavens, and Robert D. Tollison. 1986. "Final Voting in Legislatures." *American Economic Review*, September, 833–41.

Cunningham, Noble, Jr., ed. 1978. *Circular Letters of Congressmen, 1789–1839*. 3 vols. Chapel Hill: University of North Carolina Press.

Davidson, Roger H. 1980. "The Politics of Executive, Legislative, and Judicial Compensation." In *The Rewards of Public Service*, edited by Robert W. Hartman and Arnold R. Weber, 53–98. Washington: Brookings Institution.

———. 1990. "The Advent of the Modern Congress: The Legislative Reorganization Act of 1946." *Legislative Studies Quarterly*, August, 357–73.

Davis, Michael L., and Philip K. Porter. 1989. "A Test for Pure or Apparent Ideology in Congressional Voting." *Public Choice*, February, 101–11.

Dodd, Lawrence C. 1985. "Congress and the Quest for Power." In *Studies of Congress*, edited by Glenn R. Parker, 489–520. Washington: Congressional Quarterly.

Downs, Anthony. 1957. *An Economic Theory of Democracy*. New York: Harper and Row.

———. 1967. *Inside Bureaucracy*. Boston: Little, Brown.

Fenno, Richard F., Jr. 1973. *Congressmen in Committees*. Boston: Little, Brown.

———. 1975. "If, as Ralph Nader Says, Congress Is 'the Broken Branch,' How Come We Love Our Congressmen So Much?" In *Congress in Change*, edited by Norman J. Ornstein, 277–87 New York: Praeger.

———. 1978. *Home Style*. Boston: Little, Brown.

Ferejohn, John A. 1974. *Pork Barrel Politics: Rivers and Harbors Legislation, 1947–1968*. Stanford, Calif.: Stanford University Press.

Fiorina, Morris P. 1977. *Congress: Keystone of the Washington Establishment*. New Haven, Conn.: Yale University Press.

———. 1989. *Congress: Keystone of the Washington Establishment*. 2d ed. New Haven, Conn.: Yale University Press.

Fiorina, Morris P., David W. Rohde, and Peter Wissel. 1975. "Historical Change in House Turnover." In *Congress in Change*, edited by Norman J. Ornstein, 24–57. New York: Praeger.

Fitzgerald, Randall, and Gerald Lipson. 1984. *Porkbarrel* Washington, D.C.: CATO Institute.

Francis, Wayne L. 1989. *The Legislative Committee Game.* Columbus: Ohio State University Press.

Froman, Lewis A., Jr. 1963. "The Importance of Individuality in Voting in Congress." *Journal of Politics,* May, 324–32.

Garand, James C., and Donald A. Gross. 1984. "Changes in Vote Margins for Congressional Candidates: A Specification of Historical Trends." *American Political Science Review,* March, 17–30.

Gertzog, Irwin N. 1976. "The Routinization of Committee Assignments in the U.S. House of Representatives." *American Journal of Political Science,* November, 693–712.

Goldenberg, Edie N., and Michael W. Traugott. 1984. *Campaigning for Congress.* Washington, D.C.: Congressional Quarterly.

Hibbing, John R. 1988. "Washington on 75 Dollars a Day: Members of Congress Voting on Their Own Tax Break." *Legislative Studies Quarterly,* May, 219–30.

Holcombe, Randall G., and Glenn R. Parker. 1991. "Committees in Legislatures: A Property Rights Perspective." *Public Choice,* March, 11–20.

Holmstrom, Bengt. 1979. "Moral Hazard and Observability." *Bell Journal of Economics,* 74–91.

How Congress Works. 1983. Washington, D.C.: Congressional Quarterly.

Jennings, Bruce, and Daniel Callahan, eds. 1985. *Representation and Responsibility.* New York: Plenum Press.

Johannes, John R. 1980. "The Distribution of Casework in the U.S. Congress: An Uneven Burden." *Legislative Studies Quarterly,* November, 517–44.

Kalt, Joseph, and Mark Zupan. 1984. "Capture and Ideology in the Economic Theory of Politics." *American Economic Review,* June, 279–300.

———. 1990. "The Apparent Ideological Behavior of Legislators: Testing for Principal-Agent Slack in Political Institutions." *Journal of Law and Economics,* April, 103–31.

Kaplan, Abraham. 1964. *The Conduct of Inquiry.* San Francisco: Chandler Publishing.

Kau, James, and Paul Rubin. 1979. "Self Interest, Ideology, and Logrolling in Congressional Voting." *Journal of Law and Economics,* October, 365–84.

Kernell, Samuel. 1977. "Toward Understanding 19th Century Congressional Careers: Ambition, Competition, and Rotation." *American Journal of Political Science,* November, 669–94.

Kihlstrom, Richard, and Mark Pauly. 1971. "The Role of Insurance in the Allocation of Risk." *American Economic Review, Papers and Proceedings,* May, 371–79.

Kingdon, John W. 1973. *Congressmen's Voting Decisions.* New York: Harper and Row.

Klein, Benjamin, and Keith B. Leffler. 1981. "The Role of Market Forces in Assuring Contractual Performance." *Journal of Political Economy,* August, 615–41.

Kravitz, Walter. 1990. "The Advent of the Modern Congress: The Legislative Reorganization Act of 1970." *Legislative Studies Quarterly,* August, 375–99.

Krehbiel, Keith. 1990. "Are Congressional Committees Composed of Preference Outliers?" *American Political Science Review,* March, 149–63.

Kritzer, Herbert. 1978. "Ideology and American Political Elites" *Public Opinion Quarterly,* Winter, 484–502.

Landes, William, and Richard Posner. 1975. "The Independent Judiciary in an Interest Group Perspective." *Journal of Law and Economics,* December, 875–901.

Lindblom, Charles E. 1965. *The Intelligence of Democracy.* New York: Free Press.

Lipset, Seymour M., and William Schneider. 1983. *The Confidence Gap.* New York: Free Press.

Loewenberg, Gerhard, Samuel C. Patterson, and Malcolm E. Jewell, eds. 1985. *Handbook of Legislative Research.* Cambridge: Harvard University Press.

McChesney, F. S. 1987. "Rent Extraction and Rent Creation in the Economic Theory of Regulation." *Journal of Legal Studies,* January, 101–18.

McCormick, Robert E., and Robert D. Tollison. 1979. "Rent-Seeking Competition in Political Parties." *Public Choice,* 5–14.

———. 1981. *Politicians, Legislation, and the Economy.* Boston: Martinus Nijhoff.

Mann, Thomas E. 1978. *Unsafe At Any Margin.* Washington, D.C.: American Enterprise Institute.

Maurice, S. Charles. 1986. *Economic Analysis: Theory and Applications.* 5th ed. Homewood, Ill.: Irwin.

Matthews, Donald R. 1960. *U.S. Senators and Their World.* New York: Alfred A. Knopf.

Mayhew, David R. 1974a. *Congress: The Electoral Connection.* New Haven, Conn.: Yale University Press.

———. 1974b. "Congressional Elections: The Case of the Vanishing Marginal." *Polity,* Spring, 295–317.

Miller, Gary J., and Terry M. Moe. 1983. "Bureaucrats, Legislators, and the Size of Government." *American Political Science Review,* June, 297–322.

Miller, Warren E. 1964. "Majority Rule and The Representative System of Government." In *Cleavages, Ideologies and Party Systems,* edited by E. Albardt and Y. Littmen, 343–76. Helsinki: Transactions of the Westermarck Society.

Miller, Warren E., and Donald E. Stokes. 1963. "Constituency Influence in Congress." *American Political Science Review,* March, 45–57.

Moe, Terry M. 1984. "The New Economics of Organization." *American Journal of Political Science,* November, 739–77.

Niskanan, William A. 1971. *Bureaucracy and Representative Government.* Chicago: Aldine-Atherton.

Olson, Mancur. 1971. *The Logic of Collective Action.* Cambridge: Harvard University Press.

Ornstein, Norman J., Thomas E. Mann, and Michael J. Malbin. 1990. *Vital Statistics on Congress, 1989–1990.* Washington, D.C.: Congressional Quarterly.

Parker, Glenn R. 1986. *Homeward Bound: Explaining Changes in Congressional Behavior.* Pittsburgh: University of Pittsburgh Press.

———. 1989a. "Looking beyond Reelection: Revising Assumptions about the Factors Motivating Congressional Behavior." *Public Choice,* December, 237–52.

———. 1989b. *The Characteristics of Congress.* Englewood Cliffs, N.J.: Prentice-Hall.

———. 1992. "The Distribution of Honoraria Income in the U.S. Congress: Who Gets Rents in Legislatures and Why?" *Public Choice*, 167–81.

Parker, Glenn R., and Roger H. Davidson. 1979. "Why Do Americans Love Their Congressmen So Much More Than Their Congress?" *Legislative Studies Quarterly*, February, 52–61.

Parker, Glenn R., and Suzanne L. Parker. 1985. *Factions in House Committees*. Knoxville: University of Tennessee Press.

———. 1989. "Why Do We Trust Our Congressmen and Does It Matter?" Paper delivered at the annual meeting of the American Political Science Association, Atlanta, Ga., August 31–September 3.

Peltzman, Sam. 1985. "An Economic Interpretation of the History of Congressional Voting in the Twentieth Century." *American Economic Review*, September, 656–75.

Polsby, Nelson W. 1971. "Good-bye to the Inner Club." In *Congressional Behavior*, edited by Nelson W. Polsby, 105–10. New York: Random House.

———. 1985. "The Institutionalization of the U.S. House of Representatives." In *Studies of Congress*, edited by Glenn R. Parker, 81–118. Washington, D.C.: Congressional Quarterly.

Polsby, Nelson W., Miriam Gallaher, and Barry S. Rundquist. 1969. "The Growth of the Seniority System in the U.S. House of Representatives." *American Political Science Review*, September, 780–807.

Poole, Keith, and R. Steven Daniels. 1985. "Ideology, Party, and Voting in the U.S. Congress, 1959–1980." *American Political Science Review*, June, 373–99.

Price, H. D. 1975. "Congress and the Evolution of Legislative 'Professionalism.'" In *Congress in Change*, edited by Norman J. Ornstein, 2–23. New York: Praeger.

Ripley, Randall B. 1967. *Party Leaders in the House of Representatives*. Washington, D.C.: Brookings Institution.

Saloma, John S., III. 1969. *Congress and the New Politics*. Boston: Little, Brown.

Shepsle, Kenneth A. 1978. *The Giant Jigsaw Puzzle*. Chicago: University of Chicago Press.

Shepsle, Kenneth A., and Barry R. Weingast. 1981. "Structure-Induced Equilibrium and Legislative Choice." *Public Choice*, 503–19.

———. 1987. "The Institutional Foundations of Committee Power." *American Political Science Review*, March, 85–104.

Shughart, William F., II, and Robert D. Tollison. 1986. "On the Growth of Government and the Political Economy of Legislation." *Research in Law and Economics*, 111–27.

Sinclair, Barbara. 1983. *Majority Leadership in the House*. Baltimore, Md.: Johns Hopkins University Press.

Smith, Steven S. 1986. "Decision Making on the House Floor." Paper delivered at the annual meeting of the American Political Science Association, Washington, D.C., August 28–31.

———. 1989. *Call to Order*. Washington, D.C.: Brookings Institution.

Spence, Michael, and Richard Zeckhauser. 1971. "Insurance, Information, and Individual Action." *American Economic Review*, May, 380–87.

Stigler, George J. 1971. "The Theory of Economic Regulation." *Bell Journal of Economics,* Spring, 3–21.

———. 1976. "The Sizes of Legislatures." *Journal of Legal Studies,* January, 17–34.

Thomas, Martin. 1985. "Election Proximity and Senatorial Roll Call Voting." *American Journal of Political Science,* February, 96–111.

Tollison, Robert D. 1989. "Chicago Political Economy." *Public Choice,* December, 293–97.

Tullock, Gordon. 1965. "Entry Barriers in Politics." *American Economic Review, Papers and Proceedings,* May, 458–66.

U.S. Congress. 1881–1987. *Congressional Directory.* Vols. 47–100. Washington, D.C.: Government Printing Office.

U.S. Congress. House. Commission on Administrative Review. 1977a. *Hearings on Financial Ethics.* 95th Cong., 1st sess., January 13, 14, and 31 and February 2 and 7.

———. 1977b. *Final Report of the Commission on Administrative Review.* 95th Cong., 2d sess., H. Doc. 95–276.

U.S. Congress. Senate. Committee on Government Operations. 1973. *Confidence and Concern: Citizens View American Government.* 93d Cong., 1st sess., pt. 1, December 3.

U.S. Government Printing Office, *Congressional Record.* 1968–88.

United States Statutes at Large. 1881–1988. Vols. 22–100. Washington, D.C.: Government Printing Office.

Weingast, Barry R. 1979. "A Rational Choice Perspective on Congressional Norms." *American Journal of Political Science,* May, 245–63.

———. 1984. "The Congressional-Bureaucratic System: A Principal-Agent Perspective (with Application to the SEC)." *Public Choice,* 147–91.

Weingast, Barry R., and William J. Marshall. 1988. "The Industrial Organization of Congress; or, Why Legislatures, Like Firms, Are Not Organized as Markets." *Journal of Political Economy,* 132–63.

Weingast, Barry R., Kenneth A. Shepsle, and Christopher Johansen. 1981. "The Political Economy of Benefits and Costs: A Neoclassical Approach to Distributive Politics." *Journal of Political Economy,* 642–64.

Weissberg, Robert. 1978. "Collective vs. Dyadic Representation in Congress." *American Political Science Review,* June, 535–47.

Welch, William P. 1980. "The Allocation of Political Monies: Economic Interest Groups." *Public Choice,* 97–120.

Wilkerson, John D. 1990. "Reelection and Representation in Conflict: The Case of Agenda Manipulation." *Legislative Studies Quarterly,* May, 263–82.

Yiannakis, Diana Evans. 1982. "House Members' Communication Styles: Newsletters and Press Releases." *Journal of Politics,* November, 1049–71.

Young, James S. 1966. *The Washington Community,* 1800–1828. New York: Columbia University.

Name Index

Subject Index